Sunny Day Publishing, LLC
Cuyahoga Falls, Ohio 44223
www.sunnydaypublishing.com

SIGNS
In The Rearview Mirror
Leaving a Toxic Relationship Behind

ISBN 978-1-948613-01-9
Library of Congress Control Number: 2018933105

Designed by Stacie Gerrity

Printed in the United States of America
First Printing February 2018

For Molly, Raedin,
and Lexi—

May the light from the
bridges I have burned
illuminate your paths to
healthy, happy, and successful
lives and relationships.
Always be brave enough to
love yourself first.
I love you.

SIGNS

In The Rearview Mirror

Leaving a Toxic Relationship Behind

Kelly Smith

Note to Reader:

I have tried to recreate events, locations,
and conversations to the best of my ability.
This book was written from my point of view
and reflects my opinion alone.
Names have been changed to protect
people's privacy.

Chapter One

I was sitting on my couch in the living room, scrolling through Facebook. I had just gotten home from the gym and the kids were all in school. I was in the middle of my post-workout resting routine, sipping on a protein shake when I saw his face pop up as "People You May Know." I looked at his face, squinted my eyes, and then looked down at the name. Gabriel Eriksson. I opened his page to take a closer look.

"Holy shit," I thought. "He looks exactly the same as he did in high school."

I made his profile picture bigger to study his face. His hair was still a brilliant blond, but with darker shades beginning to grow in thicker and still trimmed neatly. His green eyes still that shade of deep green, surrounded by perfectly manicured eyebrows. He was wearing a blue shirt that complimented his light Swedish skin. He was sitting behind a desk with his hands folded in front of him and he was flashing that amazing smile across his face. The type of smile that catches you off guard... those dimples. Suddenly I found myself blushing.

As I scrolled through his pictures, I noticed there weren't many. I thought maybe he just joined and I was right. He had made the page about a month before he popped up on my list of "People You May Know." I went back and forth with requesting him as a friend. Back in high school he was a popular jock. He ruled the football field and dominated the basketball court. He always dressed well and seemed to be a nice guy. I did remember, however, that he had a reputation for being a ladies' man and he was rumored to have cheated on his long-term girlfriend, though I had no evidence of whether that was true or not.

As for me, in high school I was the total opposite of Gabe. I wasn't popular and I didn't dress well. My parents didn't have a lot of money and I was one of six kids. I spent most of my time after school and on weekends working and used a majority of the money to help my parents make ends meet. More of a wallflower, I didn't get a lot of attention from guys. I was skinny, had tooth decay and a head of unruly hair. Gabe was handsome, outgoing, and owned the room. So sitting there in my living room, staring at his picture, I had no reason to add him as a friend. Or did I?

May 1994, Connecticut

I was in the bathroom of my then-boyfriend's house. Derek and I met during the summer of 1993. We worked together that entire summer. Derek didn't seem to mind how I looked. I am sure I thought I looked worse than I did, and after getting to know each other, we clicked. When the summer was over, he went back to college to play football and I went back to my junior year of high school. We continued talking and eventually a relationship blossomed. Not long after, we discovered I may be pregnant. Derek was leaning on the counter and I was peeing on a pregnancy test. Not a word was spoken as we impatiently waited to see the results of the only test I ever hoped to fail. Three minutes later Derek was in tears and I was in shock, alone on his bathroom floor. I was seventeen and I was pregnant. I was a junior in high school and Derek was a sophomore in college. After collecting ourselves, we got in his car, silently drove to my house, and he left. I sat in my room that night with a heavy mind and no idea what I was going to do.

The following day I went to school and mindlessly went to my classes. I couldn't concentrate on anything. I almost made it through the day but in my 7th period accounting class I asked to go to the bathroom. I didn't make it very far before the tears started streaming down my face. I was breaking down and had no idea where to go and who I could turn to. So I didn't go anywhere. I threw myself on the floor, sat against a wall of lockers in the hallway and continued to cry. As I sat there with my hands covering my tear-filled face knowing the other students were confined to their classes, I heard a voice.

"Are you okay?" the mystery voice asked.

When I looked up I was surprised. No one was supposed to be in the hallway, least of all Gabe Eriksson. After seeing my face, without saying a word he reached for my hand, helped me up, and proceeded to walk me to the nurse's office. He led me to a room that was safe and empty, sat me down and for the next twenty minutes or so listened to me as I told this beautiful stranger all of my fears. I revealed to him that I didn't want to be with the baby's father. I told him I was frightened with no idea what I was going to do. He handed me tissue after tissue and held my hand and told me that I would be okay. When the nurse came in, he let go of my hand, wished me luck, and left. That was the last time I saw his face until it appeared on the screen of my laptop during my post-workout routine.

I sat with that memory as vivid as if it were yesterday and remembered how he had made me feel that day. He had been on my mind from time to time ever since. The first person after Derek I told I was pregnant. He consoled me during a time where I was so lost and so confused... and he didn't judge me. Without another thought, I clicked "friend" and sat back into my couch with the realization that I had just requested the friendship of the most popular guy in my high school. Suddenly I mentally morphed back to the shaggy haired, insecure nobody I was all those years ago. I was no longer the beautiful bikini competitor and fitness model I started my day as.

After finding out I was pregnant, Derek and I decided to keep the baby. We had our son and in the years to follow we did the "right thing" by getting married and soon after we welcomed two more sons. Throughout our marriage we both had resentment and anger but I will admit, most of it was from me. Growing up, I learned how to be a wife from what my mom showed me. I called Derek names, put him down and questioned every move he made. If he went to the gym I asked him who he talked to and what they talked about. I would call him 30-40 times a day at work and when he got home I was convinced he was not telling me something that may have happened while he was at his office. This went on for years and looking back on it I didn't think what I was doing was wrong. I thought it was okay. I thought it was my duty as a wife. I was taught early on that men are supposed to be treated badly by women and men just had to suck it up. I had no idea my sons were watching while pollution spilled out of my mouth and all over their dad. I thought my behavior was normal and all relationships were this way.

Derek and I loved each other, but not in a passionate way. We began to grow apart and soon it was all too much to handle and we decided to separate. In the midst of the crumbling of my sixteen-year marriage, I got a notification that Gabe Eriksson accepted my friend request. I was shocked to say the least. After hitting "send" on my page, I had completely forgotten I had requested his friendship.

Viewing his page was a good distraction from what was going on in my life. A day or so after he accepted, I received a private message from him.

"I am sorry but do I know you?" it read.

I responded telling him we went to high school together. He responded, "No we did not. I would have remembered you." After a few messages back and forth, he put the pieces together and remembered exactly who I was. He could not believe I was the same person he went to high school with. He even went as far to say that I was the swan at the end of the Ugly Duckling. He was not wrong; I had transformed myself over the years. After three kids, I gained a lot of weight. I grew sick of being heavy and I worked hard, lost weight and started to compete in bikini competitions. I was able to tame my hair, had my teeth fixed, learned how to apply makeup, and was living a life that was fit and healthy.

We began to talk frequently and discovered we had a lot in common. I was a personal trainer with a small gym in my garage. He was a trainer working in a local gym close to his house so we chatted about workouts here and there. He would post on my wall, comment on my pictures and even gave me a nickname, "Swan." Because I went from an ugly duckling to a swan.

We seemed to be hitting it off, but I was still married and going through a tough time. It even crossed my mind to stop talking to Gabe, but since he lived in Connecticut and I was now living in Texas, surely nothing could come of it, or so I thought. Innocently, I continued talking to him.

We always had something to talk about and he managed to make me laugh a lot. Laughter was exactly what I needed while going through my separation and before I knew it, I began to have feelings for Gabe. I wasn't sure if the feelings were real or if it was because he was there for me during a tough time, once again. But the feelings were there nonetheless.

I was so confused about how I felt because although I knew my marriage was ending, I still loved my husband. I wanted to fight for our marriage but I also knew he was not the right person for me. Gabe expressed his feelings for me and the seriousness of my separation set in. Gabe could tell I was distracted and that I was going through a lot. He told me to get through what I needed to and to call him when the dust settled.

Hearing that from Gabe sent me into panic mode. At the time I had no idea why. Looking back on it today it is crystal clear. I was terrified of being alone. Plain and simple. I clung to him because at the time, I felt he was all I had and I wasn't sure where my life was going. I had never been on my own before. Sobbing, I told Gabe I wanted to keep talking to him. I told him I wanted to see him... that I would fly back home to Connecticut, and I did.

Chapter Two

As we enter new relationships, we go in blind. For the most part, we trust until we are given reasons not to. That is what I did anyway.

When I met Gabe for the second time, I had no reason to not trust him. I had no reason to ever suspect him of lying about anything. I went into this not expecting much to come out of it. I lived in Texas and he was still in Connecticut. I was going through a separation and I had no idea whether Derek and I would work things out or not. But I moved forward. With an open mind and heart, I got on that plane to go see Gabe.

The morning I was supposed to go I saw on the news that they were expecting snow and I was suddenly unsure if I could go. My track record for driving in the snow was not that great. Each winter since getting my license, I had an accident. Hearing the weather forecast was exactly what I needed as an excuse to not go home that weekend. While I was in the shower that morning getting ready, I played out the conversation I was going to have with Gabe and before my final rinse, I had decided to stay in

Texas. I got out of the shower, wrapped a towel around my dripping body and texted Gabe. I told him I was an awful driver in the snow and that it would be better for me to visit another time. I put the phone down and began to dry off. Minutes later my phone buzzed. It was Gabe. His response, "Get your ass on that plane and come see me."

A giant smile appeared on my face, and with a skipped beat in my heart and the excitement of being desired in my blood, I threw on my favorite green flannel, comfiest pair of jeans and headed to the airport.

When I landed, I texted Gabe. I let him know I was there and I would meet him in the baggage area. He responded and let me know he was almost at the airport. As I got off the plane and walked toward baggage, I had butterflies in my stomach and a dry mouth. I had no idea what to expect. I was excited and I felt guilty at the same time. I was still married to Derek. We were separated, but still married and that was in the back of my mind, but slowly creeping to the front of my mind.

I arrived at the baggage claim and waited for the luggage to drop. I knew Gabe was not there yet, so I waited patiently until I spotted my bright pink suitcase. As soon as I could I scooped it up. As I moved around the airport with my roller bag behind me, I nonchalantly surveyed my surroundings to see if I could see Gabe. Just as I was sitting down, he texted me to let me know he had just got there and was on his way to meet me. I began to sweat. I had second thoughts. My hands were shaking. I had no idea what to do when I saw him, so I got up, walked over to my bag, crouched down, eventually sitting, and started to rummage through my bag looking for nothing.

All of a sudden in my peripheral vision, I saw him walking toward me. I knew it was him without looking up because he has a distinct walk. As soon as I spotted that walk, I recognized it right away. I was excited and panicked at the same time. My guilt overwhelmed me and I wanted to throw up. Again I was sitting on the floor when I heard his voice. I looked up and there he was. Blond hair, green eyes, tanner-than-usual skin, and that cologne. When I stood up, he had his arms open for me to hug him and I did. My nerves began to simmer and I started to relax as I felt his arms around me. He asked me how my flight was and we made some small talk as he grabbed my bag and we headed toward the rental car shuttle area. Because I didn't know Gabe very well I had made a reservation to rent my own car. He was dropped off at the airport by his friend, he said, and that was why he was so late.

On the bus headed to the rental car area, Gabe and I sat close together, our legs touching. His cologne filling my nostrils, the warmth of his body floating toward mine, and his presence somewhat calming mine. I looked at him and just felt safe. No idea why, but I did. We had spent a lot of time on the phone and texting. I felt as if I'd known him my entire life but it had only been a few weeks. As I looked him over I instantly liked the way he was dressed, in a green and light blue gingham button-down shirt with the cuffs folded up, jeans and those all-too-familiar penny loafer shoes. For whatever reason, I have always associated him with those shoes. And I swear he was wearing the same exact ones he wore in high school. But he wore them well. He wore all of it well.

He had that familiar smile across his face almost the entire time we sat together. When I asked him why he had that smile, he said it's because he could not believe I was actually there with him and he placed his hand lovingly on my knee. That made my heart melt and I fell deeper and deeper into the feeling that this may go somewhere. And that scared me.

As I sat close to Gabe, I thought about my marriage. I had a sick feeling come over me again, but this time the feeling lingered. I looked up at Gabe and I could not help but think about my estranged husband, the father of my three sons.

In an instant, I seemed to relive every moment over the past twenty years with Derek. Everything from getting pregnant to him losing interest in me over time. I can't say I blamed him. I wasn't so easy to live with. I was needy. Demanding. Co-dependent. I should have done more of the simple things, like help with dishes after he cooked. Let him have nights out with his friends and left him alone to enjoy his time with them. And less of the abusive things; name-calling, questioning, and degrading him in front of others just to get a laugh. Although at the time I thought I was perfect. We had years between us. So many memories, both good and bad. I thought back to day I found out I was pregnant with our oldest son, Todd, and how I eventually ended up sitting with Gabe that day.

There are particular events in your life where all you

have to do is close your eyes and you can recall everything. Every detail pops back in your head as if it is etched in steel and stored in the hard drive of your brain. It was July in my hometown of Cheshire. I was in Derek's vomit-blue bathroom. I say vomit-blue because the bathroom was decorated all in blues and what happened to me that day, in that bathroom, made me want to vomit.

I can still see the white Formica countertop with baby-blue swirls running through it. I can see the sunlight peeking through the curtain to illuminate the powder-blue bathtub and blue shower curtain. I remember thinking that it was so disgusting that his parents had books in the bathroom. The thought of his mom sitting on the toilet reading gave me visions I would never be able to forget. The aroma surrounding us was a mixture of shell-shaped soaps purchased mindlessly at the counter of TJ Maxx and the perfume his mom wore to church every Sunday. It was the only bathroom in the house, so we had no choice but to take the test in the one room that was shared by the entire family at some point that morning.

Derek was leaning against the counter and I sat on the toilet and peed on the test strip. Mind you, we didn't read the box before I peed. I guess we figured it would say yes or no, thumbs up or thumbs down, plus or negative. So I peed, put the strip on the counter, wiped and pulled up my pants. That is how long it took for the test strip to turn bright blue. The fact that it happened so fast I knew couldn't be good. And we aren't talking faint blue here. It was the bluest stick I had ever seen in my life. It was ridiculously blue, screaming blue. It was so blue that I never wanted to see that color again in my life. It was so blue that I hated Smurfs after that. That is how blue it was. It was as if that test strip had it in for me. It wanted to stick it to me and all the other teenagers having unprotected premarital sex. I was its next target.

Derek looked at the strip, his head down. He muttered, "two lines, two lines." In that moment, as he grabbed the box to read the code key, I watched as his innocence slipped away in a flash. In that last moment of freedom, he read the box, then stared at the strip and didn't say a thing. I had no idea what was going through his head at that point. I knew he was someone I did not want to be with forever. I was unhappy with him at this point and it looked like we were about to spend eternity together.

I was seventeen, a junior in high school and Derek was nineteen, just finishing his second year of college and I was pregnant with his baby. Derek dropped to the floor and started to cry. In stunned silence I held him and then, through my own tears, told him he was going to be okay. When he was able to move, he made his way to his bedroom and called his friend, leaving me on that blue bathroom floor.

When I finally thought I was able to move, I found I couldn't. Fear had immobilized me. I guess somewhere I felt that if I didn't move, stayed frozen in time, I wouldn't have to face this. Everyone could just work around me as I sat on that bathroom floor and use me as a toothbrush holder or something. That way I wouldn't have to deal with the reality of it all, or tell my parents, or think about it. Of course, I knew at some point, I would have to move. The sad part was, I had nowhere to go. No one to tell.

After Derek hung up the phone, he felt better. Not good, but better. I wondered what that felt like, to feel better. I could not remember the last time I felt better. For as long as I could remember I always had to deal with adult problems. At age twelve I was worried about the electricity getting turned off. I had to hide blankets from my siblings to be sure I was warm when the heat was turned off. We never knew exactly where our next meal was coming from. I was always in survivors' mode. And this adult problem would be no different. I would have to deal with it whether I liked it or not. I did eventually get up, put one foot in front of the other, and leave.

Derek stayed home in his comfortable room, where football posters hung from the walls with the smell of pot roast being cooked by a "normal" mother in a clean kitchen down the hall. As for me, I went to the place I called home. A place where the smoke hung so heavy in the air that the thickness of it stuck to my nose and throat. I felt the filth and grime as I walked across the old carpet in the living room housing parasites, food stains, and years of spilt drinks. I headed towards the kitchen to see piles of dirty dishes in the sink, used pots and pans still on the stove, and the disgusting pyramid of trash climbing the wall from the trash can, begging to be emptied. Through the smoke in the living room, I heard a cough and saw that familiar faint orange glow... one of my parents buried beneath the fog of their life-long obsession.

I made my way to my bedroom, easily unnoticed. I laid on my bed, the top half of the bunk I shared with my little sister, in that pit of a house, with that tiny little secret nestled in the deep dark corners of my womb. Staring at the paint peeling from the ceiling and the cracks in the walls, I thought of all the ways I could mess up a kid's life. What had I done? How could this be happening to me?

Derek and I had gone through so much together between that moment and this one, the moment where I am with someone else and not him. How did I get to this moment right now?

I was jerked out of my thoughts of Derek as the shuttle pulled up to the rental center. Gabe bounced up, grabbed my bag and helped me off the bus. As we walked, he dragged my bag behind him and opened the doors for me. This was new. And it felt good. I was missing home less and less. We stood in line waiting for our turn and we talked. We laughed and he would slightly touch my shoulder or my arm in a flirtatious way and my smile would grow. He knew what he was doing. Home was now a distant memory and I was fully in the present moment with a handsome man who wanted to be with me.

We got into my rental car. We drove to the hotel where I had made reservations. When I pulled in his car was already in the parking lot. He had dropped it off when his friend picked him up to take him to the airport to meet me.

I checked in to the hotel and Gabe was by my side the entire time with my bag safely behind him. It might not seem like much, but the way he cared for my bag made me feel wanted, appreciated. It was something I never really felt with Derek. It wasn't that Derek didn't want me or appreciate me, it was that he showed it in a different way, a way I was unable to see at the time.

When we got to my room, I opened the door and began to settle in. We made small talk as I unpacked and put my things away. We talked about him going to work the next day, me seeing my friends, and what the plans were for that night. As we talked he moved closer to me. He inched closer and was finally close enough to grab my hand. We continued to talk as his face got closer to mine. As he slowly moved in, he gently placed his hand under my chin and pulled my face closer to his. I could feel his body moving toward mine. I knew what was about to happen and I thought about stopping it. I thought again about leaving to go home. But as soon as his hand touched my face and under my chin, I let it happen. I let the feelings of excitement in my stomach loose, I let my heart race and my mind wander to all of the possibilities of what could happen, what I suddenly wanted to happen. We had our first kiss in that hotel room. Moments later, we were hand in hand happily walking down the hallway toward his car.

That night we had dinner and we talked a lot. He shared his past with me. For hours, we sat at that restaurant table taking each other in. He told me what happened to him after high school. He told me stories and I, with my eyes and ears wide open, took it all in. He told me how he got a scholarship to play football but didn't take it because his parents didn't want him to. He spoke more about his past relationships and how each one ended. I listened to how he put one of his ex-girlfriends in the trunk of his car because she was talking to another guy. Instead of alarms going off telling me to run, I put my hand on his and felt sorry he had to do that. I remember thinking that I would never disrespect him in that way.

With all of his stories, I had questions and he had answers. Nothing with him was off limits. I remembered thinking how great it was that he was so open. That he was so willing to share so much with me so soon. The way he opened up made me feel as if I could trust him, and I started to.

I have never met someone so willing to talk about his past. His past that was colored with jail time, drug sales, and domestic violence in other relationships. All the red flags were there that night, but the way he presented them, they seemed normal. He had reasons why everything that had happened had happened. Because he was unlucky. I sat across the table and felt bad for him. I believed everything he was saying because he was so "open and honest," how could I not? By the end of the night, I felt as if Gabe was the sweetest man with a string of bad luck, who just wanted to be loved and maybe I was the person to love him.

He stayed with me that night at the hotel. I told him I was not ready to take this relationship to the next level and he respected that. When he didn't try anything that night, I was impressed. He was respecting my boundaries and that made me trust him even more. The next morning I had plans to meet up with my friend at the track. I got up before he did, I got ready and I kissed him goodbye. From his groggy slumber, he told me he would call me later and would see me that night. I grabbed my keys, threw on a giant Kool-Aid smile, and with a pep in my step, I happily made my way to see my friend.

Alone in the car I had time with my thoughts. I thought about Gabe and I began to compare him to Derek. I focused on the things that were really not that important. Opening the car door. Kissing me gently. Being so open with his feelings and with his past. When I thought about Derek, I thought about him not waiting up for me at night. Shutting his ringer off while I was out and not touching my legs enough. At the time, I was more in love with the feeling of being in love than I was with reality. What really mattered in a relationship. My marriage was ending and Gabe seemed like a perfect replacement for Derek's spot.

If I knew what I know now, I would have listened to my gut when it told me to get my ass back on that plane and go back home to fight for my marriage. As I drove I marveled at Gabe's honesty. I thought about the ex-girlfriends he had and could not believe how they treated him. I could not believe how anyone could treat such a great guy so poorly. Yes, he made mistakes, but everyone does. A guy who was set up by his best friend and served jail time for something he didn't do. I was glad he was out of jail and safely in my life.

That night I had planned to stay with one of my friends, Erika. After we worked out I stopped by the hotel to gather my things and check out. When I got back to the room, it was cleaned, and I could smell Gabe's cologne slightly in the air. Packing up, I found a note he'd left me. He talked about being a male chambermaid and how he liked things clean. He went on to tell me how different I was and how great it was to be near such a beautiful, intelligent woman and that he was not used to that. He said last night was amazing and no matter what happened after this trip, he would always think highly of me. He told me he loved me and that he would see me soon. I sat on the bed and clutched that note as if it were the holy grail, and for me in that moment it was. I threw myself back on the freshly made bed and with a smile on my face, I closed my eyes for a few minutes and thought to myself, this is how it's supposed to feel.

After I packed up and checked out, I headed to my friend's house. On my way I called Gabe and he asked me if I found the note. I smiled a foolish grin and told him I did. I could hear his smile on the other end and my stomach filled with butterflies. I told him where I was going and that later that night I would be out. I told him I hoped to see him before I left. We hung up and I drove to Erika's house.

Later that night, thirty minutes after the snow began to fall, Erika and I were out at a restaurant. While I gushed over the note Gabe left for me, she gave me warnings. She was concerned because of his reputation, jail time and who he was when we were in high school. I brushed her off and she, like a good friend, said she would support any decision I made. We ate and drank and moved down the street to a bar. While Erika and I chatted, Gabe and I were texting. He asked me where I was going and he said he would meet me.

Twenty minutes after arriving at the bar, I was sitting with Erika as the snow fell heavy and thick on that early November evening, covering the streets and everything on them. The Wanted's "Glad You Came" blasted from the speakers and as I looked up I saw the door open. With snow rushing in, so was Gabe. He took his hat off, and as he stomped the snow off his feet, he scoured the bar for his target. As soon as we locked eyes, we both lit up and headed toward each other like a magnet and steel. In the moment, it was all so perfect. Gabe drove in a snowstorm just to see me. I was so enamored with him and the fact that he thought I was worth it.

The days with Gabe flew by. By the time I knew it I was headed back to the airport to go home. I said my goodbyes to Gabe with a heart full of fresh feelings and a mind full of total confusion.

I had a lot to consider on my trip back home. As soon as I got to the airport, I was on the phone with Gabe. He wanted to make sure I got there okay. He wanted to make sure I got through security okay as well, and I did. We stayed on the phone the entire time I waited to board my flight and while I was on my flight before takeoff, we texted. I loved the feeling of him wanting to know I was okay. I loved the feeling of being wanted. Derek would check on me once a day, but this for me was great. I was a dry sponge looking for love and attention, and Gabe was willing to give me what I wanted until I was swimming in it.

I had no idea I would slowly begin to drown in not only his attention, but his lies, manipulations, and everything in between.

Chapter Three

As I texted my final goodbye to Gabe, I powered down my cell phone and placed it snug in the back of the seat in front of me. I crossed my arms and stared out the airplane window. I had so many things running through my mind, mainly excitement and confusion. I had a few hours to be totally alone with just my thoughts. The plane began to move and before I knew it I was 30,000 feet in the air and I felt safe. I felt as if no one and nothing could touch me. I felt a sense of ease because for the next few hours I didn't need to make any decisions. Yet my mind raced and my heart was heavy. I closed my eyes but could not escape the visual I had of Derek.

July 1993, Connecticut

My dad had a job in downtown Hartford. Just days before I was to start working my usual job at Dunkin Donuts, he told me that he got me a job working with him for the summer. I was pissed. I wanted to go to the beach and hang out with the few friends I had, but he had different plans, matchmaking plans. Now my dad wasn't the matchmaking sort of guy. He was the sort of guy who was cranky, stressed, and constantly fighting vices that always beat him. So when he told me I was going to work with him, I fought it, but to no avail. The morning of July 6, 1993, I sat on the bus with my dad, headed to Hartford. I remember pouting the entire way, giving him nasty, "I hope the disgusted look on my face lets you know I'm pissed" looks as we zoomed by the suburbs of Hartford on our way to my first day of work. Getting off the bus and walking up the hill to Ashburton Place was something I had zero interest in. Business people zipping by, horns honking, beggars on the corner begging...

"Money for bone cancer," boomed a woman's voice.

She sat in a wheelchair holding a coffee cup with jingling change inside. I took it all in while we walked. It wasn't my first time in Hartford. I used to go as a kid on field trips. Dad would take me to see the Whalers a few times a year, so it wasn't a culture shock by any means.

When we got to our destination, we walked through the door, found his desk and he had me sit at it. I noticed a picture of me on his desk. I picked it up, looked at it and then looked at my dad. He wasn't a big man, 5'5" maybe and about 97 lbs. He mainly shopped in the boys' section of the stores for the clothes to fit him. He had a full head of salt and pepper hair, crystal blue eyes, dark skin for a white guy and a smile on his face. Smile? That's weird, I thought. Up until then I had no idea he had teeth. But that day, in his office, away from my mom, his family, pile of bills, and hungry kids, he wore a smile and for the first time, I realized that my dad was very handsome. I learned a lot about my dad that summer, but I also learned a lot about Derek. That's who he was talking to as I studied the photo and suddenly he called me over for introductions.

Derek was cute; 6'0", 200-something pounds, jet black hair, light brown eyes that were a little too close together, olive skin, and a large awkward nose planted right smack in the middle of his face. When dad introduced us, Derek held out his hand, slightly bent over and shook my hand in an odd way. When he said, "it's nice to meet you," his smile, his straight, white teeth, his perfect lips, plump and perfectly symmetrical, I swooned.

And I instantly closed my mouth because my teeth were the complete opposite. Cracked, broken. I was sporting cavities in between my two front teeth. Half of one front tooth was missing. Broken crowns in the back caused bad breath. I pulled away, suddenly feeling uglier than ever and instantly more insecure than usual. Growing up poor, combined with a mom who was busy trying to feed us, I had no idea how to groom myself, nor did I have what I needed to do so. I wore hand-me-downs from my brothers and at times my neighbor would send some to me and my sister. I had no idea what to do with the ball of red, thick, curly hair that made its home on top of my head. Makeup was and still is sort of a mystery to me. So upon meeting, I had no intention of anything becoming what it eventually became.

Over the course of that summer, Derek and I worked together every day. We had breakfast and lunch together and at the end of the day when he left before me to go home, I missed him. We talked a lot. Football, college life. I told him about my family and friends, he told me about freshman hazing at school. We seemed to have a connection. We liked each other. But was it possible for a guy like him, a college football player, handsome, intelligent, a book lover, to be interested in lowly ol' me? Turns out he was, which

I discovered on August 27, 1993.

We were in the back room at the Department of Public Safety doing our usual job of filing away gun permit applications, while Huey Lewis and the News' "I'm Happy To Be Stuck With You" blared out on the radio, when Derek and I shared our first kiss. That was it for me. I fell for him pretty hard. But that day was our last day of work. In the next few days he was leaving for football camp located three hours away. I had no idea when I would see him again. Before he left we went out to dinner, and that night he introduced me to salad and appetizers for the first time. Derek and I grew up differently. He was an only child with dinner every night. I, one of six, was not always promised dinner.

After he left to prepare for his upcoming football season at Williams College tucked away in the Berkshires of western Massachusetts, a day later, we began our courtship. We were not officially together, but we were making our way there. We wrote letters and called each other every night. When we were not talking to each other, I was talking about him. We tried to make plans to see each other, but with us being so young, it seemed impossible.

In early October, for my birthday, he made his way to my house. After a long football practice and a 3-hour drive through the dark, winding roads of the Mohawk Trail, there he stood, on my front porch. He looked so good. His jeans fit just right, his light football jacket protecting him from the chill in the early fall evening air, his smells floated around me as the wind picked up his (to this day) familiar scents. But there he stood, his dark hair, gleaming brown eyes, and that smile with his white-as-the-driven-snow teeth peeking out from his perfectly parted lips.

At the time I had no idea my future husband, ex-husband, father of my kids, and a successful businessman was standing in front of me. He would become the key to my success, my failures, my life and my kids and I had no idea he was my future. My heart raced and I was happy to see him. We had only a few hours together, so he grabbed my hand and we were off.

Nothing major for my birthday date night, just McDonald's, a movie, a birthday card, and a used sweatshirt featuring his school's name. At the time I was making more money than he so my birthday date was also my treat. I didn't mind. I was just happy to be with him. Hours later after a trip to Raspberries Records and a purchase of The Last of the Mohicans cassette tape for him, and an awful viewing of The Good Son, it was time to say goodbye. And we did. That was the beginning of what I thought was going to be something great, and I wasn't entirely wrong.

For the record, Derek wasn't a bad guy. As our relationship progressed, kids, marriage, and life got the best of us. To be fair to both of us we were young. We had not yet figured out life. We tried, but we were just not meant to be. We learned that over twenty years, three kids, and multiple dogs.

By the end of our marriage in 2012, he wasn't trying to nurture our relationship or go out of his way to show me attention or affection. He went to work each day and came home each night. He coached the boys' youth football team, played semi-pro himself and volunteered his time in the community.

We both spent our spare time focused on everything except our marriage. While he was at practice, I was at PTO meetings. While he ran the kids through football drills, I sat on the lacrosse board. We were always busy. We both worked out and occasionally we spent time together.

For me, it just wasn't enough. Derek didn't pamper me enough and wasn't romantic enough. When my birthday rolled around and he didn't meet my preconceived expectations, I would get upset and tell him he didn't love me. Looking back, I could not have been more wrong. His way of loving me was by providing a comfortable, stable and ultimately wonderful life for the boys and me. Again, hindsight is 20/20.

So, it's no wonder, when Gabe began to show me the attention I wanted, it was like a drug. It drew me closer to him, almost like a high. "He always knows exactly what to say and when to say it," I thought to myself on the plane. I was starting to believe that maybe we were meant to be together. Maybe the day he talked to me in the hallway at school when I first found out I was pregnant happened for a reason. Could it be that I got pregnant with my oldest son so I could meet Gabe and all these years later, find my happily ever after? In my head this seemed possible, and I was starting to believe that it was fate. It made sense because after all, we had so much in common and it was so easy for him to open up to me and be totally truthful. He told me that he hadn't ever been able to open up in that way with anyone. I felt so at ease around him and was also able to just be myself and he seemed to like me just the way I was. It felt so right.

As the plane descended into Texas from New England, I felt my stomach rise into my throat. Gabe was on my mind, but Derek was picking me up from the airport. I missed Gabe. I missed the way he held my hand, how he understood me and how I felt around him. I was afraid to see Derek. How was I going to feel around him? Would he be able to see Gabe in my eyes? I felt transparent and guilt-stricken.

Just before I exited the plane, I reached into my wallet and took out the note Gabe had written to me. I read it once. Then again. And one more time, before I put it away safely and exited the plane. Per his instructions, as soon as the plane landed, I texted Gabe and let him know I landed safely. I loved that he worried so much about me already. I tucked my phone into my bag and headed to collecting my luggage.

I met Derek outside at the car. The fact that he

waited for me outside instead of coming in to meet me was a sure sign that he was not changing his mind about the separation. He helped me load my bag into the car and we made small talk on the way home. Derek was still living in the house, but we were in separate rooms. That night we had a long talk and decided it was time for him to move out. This would be an opportunity for us to see how we felt without each other. I truly didn't believe we were going to actually separate. In my mind, I thought he would move out and realize how important I was to him, he would vow to change and we would work everything out. After all, he was the one who needed to change in order to fix our marriage, not me, I told myself. I was everything a man could want. Again, I could not have been more wrong.

When I shared with Gabe that Derek was moving out, I was sort of surprised at his lack of reaction. He asked a few pragmatic questions like "When is he moving out?" "Where will he go?" "Will he pay for the house? The bills?" I did my best to answer his questions and the weight of what was happening washed over me.

It was 3 AM when I hung up the phone and I sat on the floor of the bedroom that was "ours" just a month prior. I sat against the wall and I sobbed. I was scared. The fear of the unknown overwhelmed me and I had no idea what to do on my own or where to even start in figuring it out. What did my life look like without Derek? I knew he and I had problems, but would we end up divorced? Nothing was certain in that moment.

All I knew was that after seeing Gabe, I had feelings for him. Strong feelings. It was those strong feelings that help me up off the floor and into my bed that night. I covered myself with the same sheets and comforter that once covered Derek and me... and cried myself to sleep. I woke up the next day with a mean case of cry face. As I moved around the house getting the kids ready for school, I convinced myself that it would probably take anywhere between five and ten days to get over Derek and then I could move forward with a relationship with Gabe. In my defense, up to this point Derek was my only relationship and I was incredibly naive to the toll a heartbreak takes on a person. I was clueless as to how long it actually took to get over someone and having Gabe as a distraction certainly helped me get through the day.

As the days went by, the reality set in that Derek

was moving out. I got closer and closer to Gabe and began planning another trip to see him. The further away Derek got, the closer I moved to Gabe. I didn't want to be alone. I didn't want to feel the loss of Derek. I had the idea that if I rushed with Gabe, then he could seamlessly take the place of Derek. I tried so hard to fit that square peg into the round hole. But I failed. The trip I was planning was perfect timing because his brother's 40th birthday party was coming up and he wanted me to go with him to meet his family. This had to mean something: he wanted to show me off. I didn't quite know how to handle this but I was excited and flattered.

The day Derek moved out, I went to my sister's house. I couldn't bear the sight of him moving things out. He told me he would take everything he wanted and whatever was left, I could keep. After he called to tell me he was finished, I slowly made my way home. I was afraid to go in and had no idea what would be left, if anything. He did tell me that he had hired movers to help me move to my new place so I assumed he left some items.

Derek decided to sell our house and move in with his business partner and I was moving into a house of my own. Gabe told me he didn't want me to be in the same house I lived in with my ex so it made sense. Within a week, we were totally moved out, living separately, and our house was for sale. We were officially separated and I was totally lost.

The first weekend apart Derek had the kids, and I hopped on a flight to Connecticut. I was sad about Derek, but seeing Gabe was exactly what I needed. Up to this point Gabe was supportive but he didn't like when I talked to him about Derek, so I learned to avoid that topic. Instead, I talked to my friends about the separation and with Gabe all was well in my world. At the time, I understood why he didn't want to hear it and I was focused on moving forward.

This time, getting off the plane in Connecticut was different. I was filled with excitement and couldn't wait to wrap my arms around Gabe. I left my thoughts of Derek in Texas and I was focused on my time in Connecticut. When my flight touched down I texted Gabe to let him know I had landed. He responded quickly saying he was already at the airport and couldn't wait to see me. The butterflies in my stomach danced around so happily that I could almost taste their colors.

I rushed off the plane and practically ran to the baggage claim. I almost fell as I went down the stairs to meet him. I was elated to see him standing there waiting for me. A soon as I could, I threw my arms around him and hugged him tight. My eyes closed as I felt every ounce of him against my body. I inhaled his cologne and time stood still. He grabbed my waist and at the same time, he kissed my face. In that moment, I had never been happier.

We joined hands and together we looked for my bag. Hand in hand, we made our way to his car. Honestly, we could not keep our hands to ourselves. I felt amazing. I felt loved. I felt wanted. I felt things I had never felt before and I was in love with that feeling. With him close by, holding my hand, I felt safe. We got to his car and he had a bottle of water waiting for me. "It's the little things," I said to myself as I got in and buckled the seat belt. On the way to the hotel, we talked and laughed and I felt free. He had my hand in his the entire way there and each time he looked at me from his seat I melted. Those green eyes, they got me every time. They held some sort of trance over me and I let them.

That night was his brother's 40th birthday party. I was meeting his family for the first time and I was terrified. Not yet divorced, I felt what I was doing was wrong, but I did it anyway. Gabe reassured me that his family would love me. As it turns out, one of my very good friends, Erika, was married to Gabe's brother's best friend Wyatt. So I relaxed knowing she was going to be there.

As we drove to his brother's house I was quiet. I didn't know what to expect, but Gabe was amazing. He told me to just be myself and have fun. I smiled at him and appreciated how patient he was with me. As we pulled into the driveway, I started to sweat and I am pretty sure I had a small, unnoticeable panic attack.

After walking in and meeting everyone, I felt better. Erika arrived soon after and helped ease me into the party with a drink. At one point I was standing in the living room talking to a stranger. I had what was probably the second drink of the night in my hand and I stood there chatting with my new friend. I could feel eyes on me. Eyes burning a hole in the side of my head. I slowly glanced over to my left and there was Gabe. He was standing next to his dad and they were both looking at me. Gabe holding a drink of his own, wearing that smile and showing off those dimples. Suddenly my body warmed and I melted all over the living room floor. I returned a smile and his widened. His dad looked at him then back at me and he smiled. Right then and there as those familiar green eyes were set solely on me from across the room of a crowded party, I fell in love with Gabe Eriksson.

As the night grew stale and darker, the drinks flowed heavily among all the party guests (myself included). Gabe's brother, Pete, lit a bonfire at the top of the hill. Gabe and I, hand in hand, walked up the hill to join the group. Waiting for us at the fire was Erika and her husband. Erika disappeared to get a drink and I stayed with Gabe and talked to her husband. We continued to talk as Gabe made his rounds.

A few minutes later, Gabe angrily paced around the bonfire a few times, then grabbed me by the hand and quickly led me down the hill toward the house. By the time we got to the door, he was now sort of pushing me in the direction he wanted me to go, but still holding my hand, tighter. I noticed as I tried to keep my balance that his brother and dad were close by looking at us.

When we got in the house, Gabe began to yell at me. He demanded to know why I wanted to make him look like a fool by talking to another man in front of him. He wanted to know and he wanted to know now. I struggled to make sense of exactly what was happening and when I stumbled over my words, trying desperately to tell him what he wanted to hear, he began to call me names. For the first time in my entire life, a man was calling me a bitch... a whore. He was screaming at me and telling me that I had embarrassed him and myself in front of his family. I began to cry and he stormed off, leaving me standing alone, intoxicated, scared, confused and in a strange place.

As I was trying to figure out what exactly I had done wrong, I looked around and saw Pete talking to Gabe. I didn't know my way around the house so I made my way to the hall entrance, stood against a wall, slid down and cried my eyes out on the hardwood floor.

Moments later his dad found me and he sat next to me on the floor. He said Gabe was not good for me. He told me to go home and never look back. He said Gabe didn't know how to treat a woman, especially not a good one. He insisted that he would end up hurting me and that

I deserved better. As I looked at his dad, a man I hardly knew, so many thoughts rushed through my mind. Why would a dad say these things? Was he telling the truth or did he actually think I was not good enough for Gabe? I felt bad that his dad was saying these things and in the moment even though I was scared and confused, I thought I loved Gabe and loving someone means accepting them for who they are. Just then Gabe walked up to us, told me to get up and that we were leaving. "You've embarrassed me enough for one night and it's time to go," he said angrily. Both his dad and Pete tried to convince him to stay because Gabe had been drinking, but his mind was made up. He wanted to leave, so we did. We got into the car and headed back to the hotel.

Chapter Four

Gone. Gone were the days of family movie nights. Gone were the vacations where we all loaded our luggage onto the airplane and headed somewhere sunny, somewhere beachy. Gone were the late nights on Christmas Eve staying up together complaining about wrapping presents and stuffing stockings. Gone were the summer days that would turn into late evenings grilling in the backyard and jumping into the illuminated pool for a late-night swim. Gone were shows we watched together where we sat close on the couch to share ice cream and candy. Gone were the days we forced the kids to do homework and rolled our eyes at each other while we were being parents. Gone were all of our inside jokes. Memories from our earlier days and conversations about how hard we worked to live the life we had. It was all gone. They were packed up and put into Derek's suitcase and loaded in the back of his car the day he finally left for good.

Left in their place were the eggshells I would be walking on for years. The three, four and even five times I had to think before I spoke and was still put down and insulted for being an "idiot." Drunk rants took the place of TV shows and insults replaced the ice cream and candy. Name-calling replaced walks down memory lane and lies filled the space that once occupied inside jokes. I was now living a different life altogether. A life I chose. A life I could have stopped but I didn't because I was afraid of being alone.

The ride home from Pete's birthday party was awful. Scary. Gabe was mad at me and I was crying. As he drove too fast, switched lanes like a mad person and yelled at no one, I tried to figure out what I did wrong. In my intoxicated mind, I thought I must have done something for him to be this upset.

Instead of trying to figure it out, I begged him to forgive me. I told him I was sorry and I didn't mean to embarrass him. I honestly didn't think I did. I thought about the many times I was with Derek and I spoke to other guys. He never had an issue with it. But maybe Gabe was right. Maybe Derek didn't know how to say anything to me the way Gabe did? Maybe you're not supposed to talk to other men when your boyfriend is around. I sat with those thoughts stewing in my head and continued to cry because now I thought I messed things up with Gabe. "Is he going to break up with me?" No, he can't. The idea of being without Gabe, without Derek, and on my own terrified me.

I reached for Gabe's hand and he let me put my hand on his. This was something I would soon come to recognize as a sign that he was calming down. I tried to control my tears and told him how sorry I was, how wrong I was and that I would never do anything to disrespect him like that again. He squeezed my hand and pulled me in close. I made a mental note to never talk to a guy in front of him ever again. As my brain processed what just happened and justified his actions, my gut was screaming something else. "Are you fucking kidding me?" I ignored my gut that night. And for the next five years.

The next morning when we woke up in the hotel room, Gabe pulled me close. I laid my head on his bare chest and could still smell his cologne. Everything felt right again. He had his hand on my back and moved his fingers along my spine. He apologized for getting upset and blamed his behavior on the alcohol. I forgave him and apologized again. We had our first fight and we got through it. I smiled and sunk into him, relaxing and somehow convinced he was the right one for me.

A few days later Gabe dropped me off at the airport. I was headed back to Plano, Texas and was just sick over it. I knew that all that was waiting for me was an empty house. I hated being a mom without kids. I knew I would get the boys back the next day but it was always tough coming home to no one. I took solace knowing that Gabe, although 2,000 miles away, would always be close by.

As soon as he dropped me off at the airport, we were on the phone. We were texting up until the plane was going to take off. While I was thirty thousand feet in the air, that was when I was only ever truly alone. I had so much time to go over the events of the weekend and it was all I thought about. I could not believe how mad he was at me. It was only then, sober, days later and away from him, that I could really dive into what had taken place. I knew he was wrong for reacting the way he did and I knew I was wrong for apologizing to him for something I didn't do. I wasn't used to apologizing. Then again, was it really that big of a deal for me to give up just a little bit of who I was for someone I loved? It wasn't hurting anyone... or so

I thought.

Years before Derek and I separated, I was working out and building up my name in the fitness industry. I had lost 100 pounds and that seemed to impress a lot of women. A high-profile magazine ran an article on me and my success story. That began a roller coaster of events. I began fitness modeling, and in fact it was a picture of me modeling that attracted Gabe's attention to begin with. It was one of the things he had said he most admired about me.

So when I got the news I was yet again published, I was more than thrilled to share it with Gabe. Moments after I sent him the article with the very same picture that attracted him to me in the first place, my phone rang. The voice on the other end was the guy who published the book and he was calling to offer me two magazine articles. He said that I was doing well and he would love to publish my success story along with a new photo shoot. I was shocked. Everyone in the fitness industry works so hard for this moment and it is not often you get one offer, let alone two.

After we hung up I immediately called Gabe. I was

so excited to share with him my news. He answered almost instantly and sounded happy to hear from me. He was busy at work but told me to hold on so he could go to another room to hear me better. When he got back on the phone, I could have never predicted what he was about to say. Before I could tell him about the offer I had just gotten, he laid into me.

"Are you fucking kidding with that picture? You are a mother. You look like a whore. Why do you feel it's necessary to show off your body to everyone? Why do you need so much attention from men?"

I was speechless. I felt my eyes fill with tears that slowly ran down my cheeks. I suddenly felt stupid for being so excited about the magazine publisher calling me. I sat on my couch in the living room, crying silently, while he put me down for goals I had worked so hard to achieve. He ended the call a few minutes later. After I hung up the phone, I let myself fall to the side of the couch and I sobbed. I let it all out, then picked up the phone again but this time, I called Derek.

I sent him the picture and told him about the magazine offers. He said he was so proud of me and that he would buy up all the copies of the magazines. We chatted for a few minutes and I had tears running down my face again, but for a different reason. After we hung up, I felt better and I was excited again.

A few minutes later Gabe sent me a text. He told me he loved me and I looked great. He said it was hard for him to share the woman he loved with other people. After reading that, I felt happy. I felt as if he was jealous and that was sweet. I told him I loved him too and right then, made the decision to not shoot for either magazine. I loved Gabe and if he was not going to be okay with it, I was not going to do it. Again my brain agreed, but my gut shouted, "What the fuck?'

The next weekend, when Derek had the kids, I was off again to Connecticut to see Gabe. I wasn't able to spend Christmas with him, so we decided to celebrate early. He picked me up from the airport, we had dinner and headed back to the hotel. As we checked in and I got settled, Gabe asked me if I needed to take a shower. I looked at him with confusion and told him I didn't. He insisted I take one. I gave in and took an unwanted shower.

After I got out, with a towel wrapped around me, I

headed toward my bag. When I turned the corner, it was dark. He had candles all over the room with rose petals all over the bed and he was holding a box. A jewelry gift box. He threw me on the bed, told me he loved me and asked me to open it. As I sat up looking at him and all around the room, the colorful butterflies were back and I was in love all over again. No one had ever done anything this romantic for me. It was like a scene right out of a movie.

I started to tear up, put my free hand on his face and got lost in his green eyes. He kissed me and insisted I open the box. As I unwrapped the paper, Gabe looked like a little kid. He was so eager for me to see what was inside. I opened the box and looking back at me was a three-stone diamond necklace... one for past, one for present, and one for future. It was the most beautiful necklace I had ever seen and I instantly loved it. My hands were shaking as I pulled it out of the box and tried to put it on. He sat behind me and helped me with the clasp. It hung perfectly in the middle of my chest and I was over the moon in love with both him and the amazing gift he had given me. I couldn't have known then that, years later, this was the same necklace that he would be helping some other girl clasp as a birthday gift... one he would meet at work and "fall in love with"... behind my back.

That night we went to a Christmas carnival. It was about an hour or so away from the hotel, but the ride there was full of long talks and laughter. I really enjoyed being in the car with him. We liked the same music and I loved the way he handled the car. Risky, but safe at the same time.

We arrived at the park just at the last train ride of the night took off. I didn't think it was a big deal but Gabe... just sort of lost it. He raised his voice to the elderly ticket taker and I tried to pull him away as I flashed an awkward "I'm sorry" smile. My heart raced and I had no idea why he was reacting so intensely.

Moments later, after he settled down, we went into the park. The scene was beautiful. Lights covering every inch of each tree, decorations and tons of kids waiting to see Santa. The smell of fried food and cotton candy lingered all around in the frozen New England air. We pranced around the park, played bumper cars, and tried to win one of those giant stuffed animals. We giggled and huddled together trying to stay warm... it was so cold out.

Each time a gust of wind blew, I closed my eyes to protect them from the cold and each time I slowly opened them, there was Gabe, standing close by. We munched on fried dough and sipped hot chocolate. We got in line for the Ferris wheel and boarded when it was our turn. That night, as we sat at the top of the wheel looking at the park and taking in all the sights, everything that I thought was bad in our relationship suddenly disappeared. I felt happy again. Secure.

I looked at Gabe and smiled. He pulled out his phone and we took our first picture together. I rested my head on his shoulder, he put his arm around me, pulled me in close and kissed my forehead. Round and round we went. I closed my eyes and could not imagine being any happier than I was at that moment. Both tucked safely into one another. I thought what I was feeling was love. Admiration. I thought he just had some quirks, like everyone else. I didn't have much experience with relationships so I could not see that what I was feeling was attachment and not actual love. I could not see what I did not understand.

Chapter Five

As the days turned into months and life moved forward, my divorce became more and more of a reality. One afternoon, two months after we separated and while the kids were in school, Derek came over. He walked upstairs, cut through the living room and sat at the solid wood, custom-ordered dining room table we picked out together. He took his usual seat and I pulled out the chair next to him. He opened my laptop that was already sitting on the table. As he began to type we made small talk and I watched the clock carefully.

I was not expecting a call from Gabe, but I was anxious. I was afraid he was going to discover my soon-to-be ex-husband was not only in my house but sitting at my table, next to me. He would not like that.

As my hands began to sweat, Derek and I filed for divorce… together. We picked out who would have the kids on which days. Who would have them on their birthdays and for which year. I would take Christmas and he would take Thanksgiving every other year. We had to decide who would have them on every single holiday, even

Flag Day. We Americans have so many holidays.

So as Derek and I figured out where our kids would be on Martin Luther King Jr. Day, I continued to watch the clock and my phone. We discussed health insurance, car insurance, and who would pay what for the kids. He did the math in his head and I felt nostalgic because I loved that about him. He sat there with his eyes closed as he crunched numbers in his head and I just wanted to reach out to him one last time. I wanted to tell him I still loved him and wanted us to work, but I didn't. I knew we no longer wanted the same things out of life. He spat out a few numbers, jotted them down and we moved on to other things.

We sat next to each other for about an hour and dismantled the life we spent over twenty years building. And just like that, it was done. Over. Filed. We were getting divorced. Derek and I, who had our oldest son as teenagers, homeless and on welfare, who had managed to somehow build up a thriving staffing company, have three amazing kids, become pillars in the community and volunteers extraordinaire; we were over. Our annual 4th of July celebrations were no more. Our weekly game nights with our neighbors who turned into great friends were finished.

We faced the end of our family as we knew it, and we were both lost. Confused. Sad. Now what? We had no idea how to move forward except that we still had three great kids who needed us both. Maybe now more than ever. We had to co-parent. At this point they were our main priority. We were both facing death. The death of our marriage and of our family in the only way we knew it. We even discussed that if we were indeed meant to be... we would one day find our way back to each other.

That day after Derek left, I made my way to my bedroom, crawled onto "our" bed and cried. I mourned the end of the only thing that was ever familiar to me. The only thing that was ever home to me. Derek and I, in a sense, grew up together. We had to figure out a lot of life while we were together. Now, I was on my own.

But then again, I had Gabe to lean on. I knew I had to call him before he began to wonder where I was. I sat up in my bed, wiped my tears, cleared my throat, and called Gabe. I told him we filed and now we had the two-month "cooling off" period and then it would be done.

I had a strong, cold can't-wait-for-it-to-just-be-over voice while I talked to Gabe. The truth was I was dying inside. I wanted to tell Gabe how sad I was. I wanted to be able to open up to him and let him know I was hurting. I wanted him to take care of me and tell me everything was going to be okay... but I didn't tell him what my heart was feeling. I didn't think he would understand. I was not sure he was even capable of comprehending what I was going through. After we hung up, I threw the covers over my head and cried until I had to pick up the kids.

I had a lot of moments like that. A lot of telling him great things about my days and what I was busy with, while in reality I was falling apart. The five to ten days I thought I needed to get over Derek were turning out to be a lot longer and a lot more intense. I called Derek a lot. I cried to him a lot. He would take my calls and try to help me through it. He would respond to my texts and take me out to dinner to see if I was doing okay. I could tell Derek how I felt. I could tell Derek I missed him. I could fall apart with Derek... but not with Gabe.

So, I began to see a therapist. I knew I needed help getting through this. I knew Derek and I were not good together and that I wanted to be with Gabe, but I could not figure out why I was still so sad. Gabe had no idea how much pain I was in. To this day, he has no idea how much I was suffering with the end of my marriage while trying so hard to begin something with him at the exact same time.

A few times I thought about ending it with Gabe, but then I would panic. I would be alone and that scared me. I thought it would be better to suffer than to be alone. Suffering seemed to be my hobby at this point. The only thing I knew how to do and I did it well.

Between dealing with my divorce and my relationship with Gabe, I was a complete mess. While I was working through being on my own and trying to figure out who I was, Gabe was almost imperceptibly changing. He was asking a lot of questions. Questions Derek never asked, but the questions I used ask Derek: Where are you? Who are you with? Why didn't you take my call? Who do you talk to at the gym? Why do you find it necessary to work out?

Since he worked as a personal trainer at the gym, he said he knew what really goes on at the gym and he didn't like it that I was there so much. It became too much for me. All of the arguing with Gabe was no longer worth it... so I gave up the gym. I began to eat fast food, cookies, pie... you name it. I was indulging daily in everything I was taught not to eat while I was competing and modeling. Life was easier this way. No distraction being healthy, more time to be there for Gabe when he needed me.

I began to add weight, but I figured as long as I could still see my lower abs, I would be fine. I was convinced it would only take a few weeks to get off the excess weight. I thought this was only temporary. I figured as Gabe and I got closer, he would begin to trust me. He would eventually see that going to the gym was no big deal. He would trust me and see that when I was at the gym I was there just to work out. I could hold out for a while until he changed his mind. I'm still waiting.

I was traveling back and forth from Texas to Connecticut twice a month and when I was home in Cheshire, I was eating and drinking. I no longer cared about working out and Gabe insisted that he loved the way I looked.

But deep down, I felt sad and gross. I missed my

workouts and my eating routine. But because it was less stress on my new relationship, I pushed those feelings down and covered them with burgers and fries.

The only place I felt safe was when I was 30,000 feet in the air. Only then could I be myself, let it all out, and cry. Gabe could not reach me and I didn't have to pretend to be happy. The days I volunteered at the school slowly fizzled and soon I wasn't helping out at the school anymore. I was slowly becoming a shell of my former self.

I would later realize I was falling into a deep depression. I was either crying over the end of my marriage and my family or I was explaining myself to Gabe. Things started to get dark for me and the walls were closing in. I became unrecognizable to myself.

One afternoon, after the kids left for their dad's house, I was talking to Gabe. After the call ended, I found myself on the bathroom floor, barely able to hold my head up. I was gone... so was my will to live. I rummaged through my pill bottles and swallowed as many as I could. I could not do it anymore. I could not take it anymore. I had no direction. I had no desire. I felt that I had nothing left. I felt I had no choice. I laid on the cold tile floor wondering what I had just done but not able to muster up the strength to react.

Luckily, not long after, a friend who was in the neighborhood dropped by to say hello. She found me there, limp on the bathroom floor, picked me up and managed to help me vomit. Needless to say, I failed at my attempt. Neither Gabe nor Derek, much less my kids, knew I wanted to end my life that day. It isn't until now that they may learn of how gone I really was.

It was a tough time in my life but I managed somehow to get through it. I kept seeing Gabe and putting up a strong front when he was around. I put up that front because I knew Gabe wouldn't understand. I was not protecting him from anything. I was protecting me from him. I didn't want him to know I was sad. He wouldn't have liked it very much and it was just easier to pretend to be okay than it was to be honest with him about my feelings. He would not understand that I wasn't still in love with Derek, but I was mourning the loss of my marriage. I was just sad.

So I faked it. I faked being happy with the way my life was going. Truth be told, I felt defeated, destroyed. I was in pieces and I needed some time to feel and recover from the end of my marriage. I needed to be on my own to figure out who I was. I needed time to just be with my kids and be there for them. I didn't take time for me or for my kids. I chose to put Gabe first. I chose to talk to him and listen to him bitch about his day rather than read to my sons or watch a movie with them. I chose to explain every single move I made to him over sitting close to my boys to make sure they were okay. I made those choices and I regret them to this very day.

My kids needed a healthy mom more than I needed a man. A man who made me anxious and paranoid if I missed his call. A man who called me names and put me down when I was suicidal. A man who was so concerned about himself that he never once asked me if I was okay. A man who was so upset about my social media page that I had to go through and delete every guy friend and every picture I had of me, Derek, and the kids. I was not ready to do that but I did it to please him. I deleted it all just to make things "easier" in my relationship with him.

I had a choice in all of this and I chose him over everything, myself included. I didn't love myself. I didn't know how. I was lost and confused and I was weak. I thought at the time that what I was doing was right. But it wasn't.

Chapter Six

I can't pinpoint exactly when it happened. Or even when it started. But somewhere between the romantic texts and calls, gifts and door openings, Gabe morphed into who he really was. Over time and in his own sloppiness, pieces of him began to show.

Each time a piece of the real Gabe began to peek through, he quickly diverted my attention and I thought I was imagining things. But I wasn't. He was just good at what he did. He was good at his craft. He had years and years of practice before seeking me out.

Looking back on it today with fresh eyes and a healthy mind, I can see it began the day we started talking. He was who he was from day one and I could not see what I did not recognize.

In the beginning, while he was "courting" me, we discussed deal breakers and what our turn-offs were. I was not attracted to men who smoked and I could not be with anyone who did. He told me he didn't smoke, but he used to and quit because it was a "gross habit." We talked about our families, our past relationships, and everything in between. I told him about my dad and how he passed away at 50 because he was an alcoholic who never took care of himself. I told him how awful it was growing up with an alcoholic dad who was also addicted to gambling.

My dad's and my relationship was a love-hate relationship in a way. I hated him for his horrendous temper and the mean things he said to me and my siblings over the years. I hated the demons he was fighting; the gambling, the alcoholism and the way he allowed my mother to beat him down in public. I hated the way I had to step over his lifeless, drunk body lying in our hallway on Thanksgiving Day to go to the dinner table. But he was a victim of his own upbringing and circumstances. He came from poverty and a dysfunctional family. And he married my mother not knowing he was just her escape plan from the hell she thought she was living in. Her definition of hell was not being able to smoke and drink in the house before she was eighteen, and having to stick to a curfew.

At the same time, I loved my dad so much. I never doubted that he loved me and I always knew he wanted the best for me. And he was a hard worker. God was he a hard worker! Though he always seemed to have a hodgepodge of entry-level jobs, he worked several at a time and was the person who taught me my work ethic. And he did the sweetest things sometimes. We had a little ritual: sometimes he would wake me up when he got home from work and make hot chocolate by melting a Hershey's bar in milk and we would sit at the kitchen table and talk, just the two of us, for hours. (I found later that he did this with all my siblings... the bastard!)

No one could break my heart like my dad either. I'll never forget the day when I was ten and he was home when I arrived home from school. He told me he had been laid off. I tried to comfort him in my ten-year-old way, offering some lame solution, thinking I was helping. He called me "asshole." I cried so much. He killed a piece of me that day.

Another time he came home completely drunk (again) so my mom packed us six kids up and took us to a neighbor's house. When he woke up the next morning, we were all gone. I guess that finally scared him, because that is when he checked himself into rehab. He was gone for thirty days and it was so hard for me to not have him there. I would rather have had him as a shithead at home than not home at all. He was the man that was supposed to be strong in my life, protect me, and tell me what to do.

Seeing him in rehab really made me sad. But not for the reasons you might think. He seemed so happy there, away from us. Away from her. He was never happy like that at home.

Living with him was living with a man who forced us to walk on eggshells. Showed up randomly drunk; didn't follow through with anything he promised. He made me look like a fool when we went car shopping after I got my license. I picked out a car, told my friends, and ended up with nothing.

I refused to go back to that type of pain. So I wanted to be sure Gabe was not like my dad before I let him into my life. Gabe told me about his parents and the abuse he endured while growing up. He said he didn't like the environment he was raised in and because of the way his mom yelled, he hated to be yelled at. He told me about his drinking habits from years ago and how he didn't do that anymore. He also revealed that he used to gamble, but it was too risky now.

At the time, this was all music to my ears because Gabe was a changed man who had learned from his mistakes. Derek never had any of those vices. He liked ice cream and coaching our boys' teams. This was a whole new kind of relationship and although different, I assumed it would be fundamentally the same. I assumed every guy would put my needs first, like making sure I ate when I was hungry so I didn't get hangry. I assumed I could make fun of and put any man down and he would accept it. I thought I would have the same lifestyle with vacations and shopping sprees like I did with Derek. As Gabe and I talked and I learned more and more about him, I felt better during my discovery phase. Little did I know my "discovery phase" would continue long after our relationship would end. The years and years packed full of lies, the real Gabe and the skeletons in his closet would eventually reveal themselves.

As the time passed, I realized quickly my discovery phase was not over. During a visit home, I drove past the gym where Gabe worked. As clear as day, I saw him standing outside smoking with one of his coworkers.

The cigarette went from his mouth to his side and back up again. I watched him smoking as I sat in traffic. Now, because I knew I had been a bit of a tyrant with Derek, I didn't want to be a crazy person and freak out on him. Instead, I texted him and I asked him if he was outside smoking.

His response was that he would never smoke, calling it "a filthy habit." Wow, I thought to myself. He just lied to me and... so easily. I saw him, with my own two eyes, put a cigarette to his mouth and he just told me he didn't. With further questioning, he eventually 'fessed up that he did smoke, but only when stressed because it helped "relieve the stress." After finding this out, I thought back to our conversation about it when we first met. I thought to myself, "Okay, so he smokes when he's stressed, that's not so bad. At least he's not a gambler and doesn't drink very often."

Later that night, I picked him up from work and we talked about his smoking and the fact that he blatantly lied to me. This is when I learned that he didn't like being pressed with questions and in fact, it made him very angry. I began to notice a trend: he got angry very easily and often. I could not understand why he just didn't tell me in the beginning that he was an occasional smoker. He didn't like those sorts of questions either, so when he began to yell, I backed down.

Weeks later, after I was back in Texas, I began to realize how much he drank. There was a pattern with him going out after work. At first, it didn't happen all that often. While he was at work we'd talk and text throughout the day and by the time he was off, he was in his car and I was on the phone with him. We'd talk all night.

And then, slowly, he started to call me less. Our conversations were shorter and his after-work bar visits increased. While he was out, he would still text or call occasionally, but more often than not, he would ask me to call him at a certain time to remind him to leave the bar and go home.

Eventually, my calls went unanswered or he'd pick up and yell at me for bothering him, hang up on me, and then not take my calls. The next day he'd apologize and express how bad he felt, stay home for a few nights, and then repeat the cycle. He had a pattern and I was beginning to become very familiar with it.

One night, while I was home in Texas with my kids, he called to let me know he was going out. He again asked me to call him at midnight to remind him to go home. I reluctantly agreed and when I called, he got mad and hung up on me. A few hours later, my phone rang and Gabe was on the other end of the line. He was panicked. He had been pulled over and had no idea what was going to happen. The call was cut short and I didn't hear back from him that night. That was the night he was arrested with a DUI.

The next morning when he called, he was a complete mess. He was crying because he was already on parole and was terrified that this would be a major violation that would send him back to prison. While we were on the phone, my heart was breaking for him. I was so upset and so scared. I immediately booked a flight for the next day so I could be there with him when he went to see his probation officer.

He had previously been in jail for five years because his best friend James set him up by placing drugs in his house for the DEA to find. He was sentenced to sixteen years but got out after seven for good behavior. I would come to discover the truth about what really happened and the role he really played in ruining other people's lives.

That day, I dropped the boys off at Derek's, hopped on a flight to Connecticut, and tried to comfort a pathological liar for the next ten days. I held him as he cried and he promised over and over he would never drink again. How this was all "too close to home" and he should have never been out partying.

Over the next few months, I paid for the lawyer Gabe needed to defend his case. Luckily, he didn't have to go back to jail, but he did have to attend classes for alcohol treatment and submit to drug testing more often by his parole officer.

After he got comfortable in his classes, he got comfortable going out after work again... and reacquainted with drinking in bars. I was absolutely floored when I found out. I had just spent thousands of dollars on a lawyer and he was back to calling me a bitch for giving him the reminder he so sweetly asked for just a few hours prior. Back to binge drinking and even more frightening... driving home afterwards.

I wanted to protect him. I wanted to save him. I thought if anyone could love the darkness out of this man, it would be me. There were times when I saw such goodness in him. Once, when my grandmother was sick and in a nursing home back home in Connecticut, my mom called me from her mother's room in a state of panic. She was worried about my grandmother and didn't want to be alone. I told Gabe what was going on with her and minutes later he was in his car headed to comfort my mom. He sat with both my grandmother and my mom until she was stable. He talked to them, made them laugh, and held their hands. I felt better and my mom did too. He then began to go visit my grandmother in her nursing home. She had no idea who he was, but she had a smile on her face when he entered the room. He visited weekly and for Christmas he gave her an angel that sat on top of her dresser. It lit up different colors and she adored it.

I remember one day driving on the highway, when a car nearly hit me and I almost swerved off the road. I called Gabe upset and shaking. He talked to me calmly, had me pull over and asked me to check for something in the trunk. As I got out of the car and looked in the trunk, he told me there was nothing in there and he'd just wanted me to breathe.

There was a good man deep down and I saw a light in a very dark place. I thought, "If I love him enough, the light will shine brighter and he will be okay." We will be okay. I tried for years and finally I had to give up. As I incessantly tried to search for that dim, dull light inside of him, my light smoldered and eventually extinguished. I could feel it burning out, but I thought I would be okay. I thought I could be enough for us both.

Gabe didn't want to be saved. He felt there was nothing wrong with the way he talked to me. A few months into our relationship, we were at his parents' house. He was living with them at the time because financially he could not get on his feet. He got into an argument with his parents and I remember my stomach turning and feeling sick listening to the way he spoke to his mom. The names he called her. And when his dad tried to step in, Gabe got even more verbally abusive. I remember thinking, "wow, surely he would never talk to me that way." Man, was I wrong.

I learned that if things were not going his way, he

got upset, aggressive, and angry. The best thing to do was to keep him calm and happy, which was almost a full-time job in itself. A job I happily accepted because of the good I thought he had in him. I took pride in the fact that his friends said I could handle him better than anyone else. At the end of each day, I was exhausted from being a mom, figuring out my new life and, in a sense, being Gabe's "handler." I was trying to keep him out of trouble and for the most part I was successful. If I looked away for even a few minutes, he derailed and his emergency became my fire drill as he called crying about the trouble he was in and insisting "it wasn't my fault." Nothing was his fault. Ever.

Chapter Seven

With tear-filled eyes, a heavy heart, and mild hatred for myself lingering in the back of my mind, I write this chapter. It has been a difficult yet therapeutic process for me. When I first started thinking about this book months ago, before pen ever touched paper, I was afraid of my own feelings. I was scared that I would start feeling something for him again. I was afraid I was going to miss him or fall back "in love" with him. But this process has had quite the opposite effect on me.

As much as I would love to tell you that he and this relationship were settled in my mind, they aren't. The tears are real. The pain is thick and it's heavy. The tears and pain are not for him, but for me. As I write, I realize I love the girl I am writing about. Five years ago, I didn't. Twenty years ago, I didn't. When I was growing up, self-hatred was a learned skill and all that I knew, especially when I didn't know who I was. I had no idea of the anger that lived deep within and the magnitude of the toll it took on me.

Today, after years in my recovery program, I see this

amazing, strong, intelligent, happy, fun-loving mom and woman. I am here for a reason. I have this writing gift for a reason. I lived the life I did for a reason. I am here to write for me and for you. The one who needs it most. The one who is confused and scared. I write this for you.

From the moment you find out you are pregnant, you have a responsibility to the life living within you. You are responsible for eating well, not drinking alcohol, and not inhaling fumes from the cars driving in front of you. As your belly grows, for most of us, so does the love we have for the little unknown stranger living inside us. We talk to the stranger and somehow fall in love and become totally connected. After they are born it's a motherly instinct to protect them and care for them. To make sure to pass on the important life lessons and keep them safe, no matter what.

When I found out I was pregnant with my oldest son, Todd, I was seventeen and not interested in being a mom. As the months passed, I became more familiar with this stranger and I found myself enamored with him. While Derek was away in college, I would lay in bed and talk to the "stranger" living inside me. At the time, I had no idea if he was a boy or a girl so the conversation was gender-neutral.

One night after my school day was over, homework was done, and my shift at the donut shop finished, I finished reading the baby one of my favorite Dr. Seuss books. I asked the "stranger" a question and asked the baby to kick to answer me. We talked about hockey. Football. Whether it was boy or a girl. After a few kicks here and there, I determined that said baby would play hockey when he/she grew up. To this day, Todd is not much of a liar and now, at the age of twenty-two, he's the captain of his college lacrosse team. I guess lacrosse is pretty close to hockey, so it all worked out.

That night, over twenty-two years ago, sitting alone in my bed talking to this little stranger, we formed a bond. The day he was born, I gazed into those tiny brown eyes surrounded by the softest, pinkest skin and I apologized for being his mom. I told him I would do the best I could for him and I did. Derek and I both did. That was until I did not. Until I gave him and his two brothers all-access passes with front row seats to what an abusive relationship looks like, with their mom as the leading lady.

The divorce was finalized in April. Five months and three days from the day Derek moved out and our relationship ended. That summer was the first time we did not plan a family vacation. I looked into a beach house for me and boys to stay in for a ten-day getaway. I wanted to go home to Connecticut to have them see our extended family. It was just a bonus that Gabe would be there, and an opportunity for him to get to know the kids better. I planned with Derek to figure out the details of when he would take a vacation with them and when I would.

A few days later I had the trip booked and the kids were excited to go to Connecticut for a vacation. After the ten days with me on the shore they were to fly directly to California to be with Derek for another ten days. I planned to stay with Gabe while the boys were with their dad on the west coast and then meet them back in Texas. The plan was perfect. I was excited to have what I thought of as our first family vacation all perfectly planned... but of course, I was wrong. I was still in denial of who Gabe really was and by executing this plan, I chose to put my kids directly in the line of fire. A decision I regret to this very day.

The morning we left Texas, we flew into Hartford airport and got our rental car. The plan was to go see my friend Julia. After I picked Gabe up, we drove to Julia's house. She had extra bedding and was going to let us borrow it for the duration of our trip. I can't remember exactly what happened that set Gabe off, maybe I was late, maybe I gave him the wrong directions, but he was angry at me. As we pulled up to Julia's house my stomach was in knots. My mouth was dry and I had no idea if he was going to be upset with me in front of her or if it was just a private show for me and my kids to experience.

As he got out of the car, he was cheery and chipper. He thanked her for allowing us to use her bedding. Julia made a face at me because right away she knew. She knew something was off. She had been dying to see the boys and wanted to hug them and talk to them, but Gabe was clearly on a mission to leave. As he hurried things along, she covertly grabbed my hand in support. We drove away from her house and as she became smaller and smaller in my rearview mirror, I broke a little inside.

We went to the grocery store, gathered what we needed and were off to the beach house. But even a small task like a trip to the grocery store turned into an excruciating event. He seemed to find fault with everything and everyone: how slow the line was moving; the checker wasn't emptying the cart fast enough. He was infuriated. When we finally got to the house, I figured it would all settle down. There was Gabe, out in front, putting on his nice-guy charm with all the neighbors, his usual. Meanwhile, a storm was brewing inside.

Boys will be boys. They left their bags on the floor and bounded toward the beach to see the water. Gabe took issue with their "mess." He said they were slobs and asked how could I as a mom let them live that way. I immediately defended them and told him they were excited to be at the beach and they didn't need to be neat while on a vacation. I did not understand why he was so bothered. To keep him calm, I called the boys back and had them put their stuff away. They were not super happy with this, but they did it.

Gabe had rules. He wanted everything planned. He wanted everything clean and in order all the time. No excuses. I didn't raise my kids that way and they had enough on their minds with the divorce. I figured a beach vacation would be fun. Mindless. Good memories.

During the day, Gabe worked and then came to the house afterwards. We would go to the beach, swim and fly kites. At times, we went to the arcades, played games and stuffed our faces with junk food. Fried dough, cotton candy and beach pizza. We went on rides and played games. The kids collected tickets from Skee-Ball and cashed them in for a harmonica, the same way I did when I was a kid. We drove to the go-cart track and raced each other. Some nights, we made bonfires and roasted marshmallows on the sand. We talked, joked and laughed.

Other nights Gabe walked in carrying his bad day on his shoulders and alcohol on his breath. That was a sure-fire sign that it wasn't going to be a good night. When I sensed a bad day, I cleaned the house the best I could and left the kids by themselves at the beach so I could come in and make sure everything looked perfect. But I was never able to get the house clean enough.

A few nights in he came to the house and began inspecting as soon as he walked in. He saw things he didn't like and scolded me. Beach sand on the floor (go figure), food on the counter and not in the cabinet, and clothes not put away.

One night, after inspecting, as he rolled up his sleeves to clean, the kids came in. He started to throw things in the kitchen. I sat on the couch with my stomach in knots. My blood was hot and my kids were standing in the doorway wearing their brightly colored swim suits and holding beach buckets full of sand and shells. Their tanned, smiling faces turned red and their sandy feet didn't move. They watched as he yelled, cussed me out and told me I was a "bitch" and a "pig." He asked, "how can you live this way?" He shouted that he had just worked all day and had to come home to this... that he was miserable. He had no idea what he saw in me and declared he could not ever live with me if I insisted on living this way.

I sat there frozen in embarrassment and disbelief. My kids stood in shock. The smiles they were just wearing turned into sadness and they had no idea what to do. Slowly, one by one, they sat down close to me. I held my one son's hand and he squeezed it, hard.

After about an hour, Gabe calmed down and emerged from the bedroom asking "who wants to go get pizza and play games?" I instantly felt relieved. This storm was over and he was back to normal... at least for the moment. I learned to enjoy the little moments like this while he was happy but I was always worried when and where he would flip that switch again.

The rest of our vacation was pretty much the same. Another night he showed up at the house, freaked out, and then just left. I sat outside in front of the house and cried. I called Derek. He answered and immediately, he knew something was wrong. He told me I would be okay. He told me I didn't have to be with Gabe and that I didn't deserve to be treated this way, but in the back of my head (and years later I would discover) I stayed partly because I felt I did deserve to be treated this way... but my kids didn't deserve it. They didn't deserve it at all.

More times than I care to admit, my kids witnessed Gabe abusing me. They heard him call me names. They picked me up off the floor when I was sobbing. They held me when I could not hold myself up. They saw me fall. Their hearts broke for me over and over and I just could not see what was really happening. I could not recognize that they were enduring secondhand abuse. They were scared for me and so very confused. They hated Gabe and the way he treated me but they were also afraid of him. Afraid of what he might do to them if they stood up for me. Afraid of what their dad would do if they told him any of this. So, they didn't say anything and they didn't do anything. They stood by watching their mom fall apart and they suffered, silently and alone. My boys suffered because I was not strong enough to remove myself from this abuse. Not strong enough for me. I let this happen to them and I may never be able to forgive myself because I didn't protect them from him. I did eventually get out and away, but the damage had already been done.

They may have seen me fall, cry on the floor, insulted and bruised, but they are also now seeing me rise from the wreckage. They are seeing me stand up, proud and tall. They are seeing me help others. They have witnessed me fight and become the strong woman I am today. A woman who can take care of herself. A woman who has met abuse face to face and won. I fought for me but I also fought for them.

Whether the kids were his or not, they should never see their mom (or dad) being abused in any way, shape or form. Kids, even from infancy, know exactly what is going on. They do not deserve to be in the middle of such toxicity. If you or anyone you know is in this sort of relationship, know you do not have to stay because you have kids. You are teaching them it is okay to be treated this way. Please, I implore you not to let them grow up thinking this sort of relationship is normal or even acceptable. They deserve a happy life without secondhand abuse. By staying, enduring and "taking it," you are allowing their minds to be distorted, just the same way I did.

Chapter Eight

A few months before that rainy, stormy night in Maine when we got engaged, Gabe and I talked about marriage. About him moving to Texas. About him looking for a job at a big-name gym that would not have an issue with him being a felon. Texas is tougher on felons than Connecticut is. We had so many moving parts to get through in order for him to be able to move here to Plano. He had to get permission from not only his parole officer, but also from the state of Texas. Which would prove to be a difficult task.

Parts of me wanted to marry him. Lock him down and continue my lifelong project of healing and fixing him through my unconditional love and people-pleasing skills. But there was also another part of me, a bigger part of me, that wanted to run. That wanted to pretend we never existed. So when he told me he bought a ring and was showing everyone, I got nervous. I felt trapped in a way. But I also felt excited. I was excited that he wanted to marry me. Gabe the untamable wanted to settle down with me. He wanted me as his wife forever. But what did that mean? Would he change? Would he be a better husband than he was a boyfriend? I remembered when Derek and I were together I thought the same thing.

When Derek and I got married, we had a small wedding with a handful of people. The ceremony was in the backyard of his parents' house. Todd, two and a half, was the ring bearer. As we said our vows, Derek could hardly get through them he was crying so much. In that moment I felt as if Derek really loved me and that he was going to be a better husband than he was a boyfriend.

After the ceremony, we went to a local restaurant for our "reception." No DJ. No dancing. Nothing like a typical wedding. Derek and I at the time had two jobs each and no money and so could not afford much. We were big on paying our own way. I thought the title of "husband" would somehow make Derek grow up and feel something more for me. When we made it to the restaurant, I was surprised to see Derek paying more attention to his friends than to me. I wondered when it would "kick in." I wondered when the title of husband would begin to sink in and he would sprout feelings for his wife. Well twenty-plus years, three kids, and a divorce and I am still waiting.

So maybe Gabe would not change, but on the other hand, maybe he would. Plus I had come this far and I wanted to see it through.

By the time I found myself rushing to the airport to go home that weekend, the weekend I thought maybe he was going to propose, I had already seen pictures of the ring. Gabe was excited about it and he was awful at keeping secrets; well the good secrets anyway.

Having an idea that this was going to be the weekend he was going to pop the question, I knew I had to go shopping for the perfect outfit. But I came face to face with the ugly truth while standing in front of the dressing room mirror in Target one afternoon.

When Gabe and I met, I was a size four and the days before I was planning to go home and get engaged, I was now a fluffy size twelve. Standing in the mirror of the fitting room at the store, I sported black slacks and a grey sweater. I was frumpy. I looked dumpy. I suddenly missed my baked chicken and brown rice. I sighed and realized I looked more like I was going on a job interview and less like I was about to have my entire life changed. Not able to look at myself like that again, I changed back into my sweats, scooped up my new outfit and headed to the register.

At the airport and through security, with my interview outfit tucked safely in my carry-on, I took my usual seat in the standby section. I had been a standby passenger for most of our long-distance relationship, so I knew I had to be there early and I also knew there was always a good chance I would miss my flight, so I had to be prepared. That night I missed my flight. There was bad weather and the flights were full. In order to make it home and not disappoint Gabe, I had to buy a ticket on another airline, which was not cheap. I remember talking to the lady at the ticket counter and telling her I had to get home because I thought my boyfriend was going to propose. While saying the words out loud, my stomach turned. I was being fake. Again. I was pretending to be happy when I knew it was not the right thing to do. I was pretending because now, eighteen months in, it was all I knew. By this time in our relationship I was lying to my friends, family, and myself.

"Everything is great. Gabe is amazing. We had things to work on and he has really stepped up," I lied. To everyone. Always.

Out loud and in front of people in my life, Gabe was great and I was happy. But on the inside, I was drowning. I knew something was off, but I had no idea how to end things. I did love him. My love was real. But I hated how he spoke to me. I hated how he called me names. I hated how I retaliated and called him names back. I hated how jealous I became. How angry I was. The words that started to fly out of my mouth toward him were not words I would normally say. I was changing but since it seemed okay with him, it all began to feel "normal." He would call me names, I would call him names, one of us would hang up on the other, and hours later we would be fine. We broke up and got back together so often I expected it. So why was I in such a rush to get on a flight to say yes to someone I didn't want to marry? Because it was what I did in our relationship.

I booked my flight and I texted Gabe. He was happy and relieved and so was I. I had a seat and in thirty minutes I would board my flight and I would be off to be engaged to Gabe Eriksson. I sat in my seat and daydreamed about all of it the way women do. How he would ask. How I would answer. When and where we would get married and how I would tell everyone.

How would I tell everyone? Not many people in my life liked Gabe. How could they? They saw me cry. They heard the stories. They saw how I reacted when he called me. On a visit back to Connecticut a few months prior to this, I was having lunch with two of my friends. When my phone rang and it was Gabe, I fumbled the phone in order to not miss his call. When he asked me to come to his gym, my heart sank. I asked my friends what they thought he wanted. They could see and hear that I was afraid of getting in trouble.

The entire way there I was worried. My stomach was in knots and I kept reliving the past few hours since I dropped him off to see if I could remember anything I did. When I pulled into the gym my heart was racing so much I thought I was going to pass out. It turned out he wanted to surprise me with roses. After we pulled out of the gym my friends were now more worried than they had ever been. They didn't like to see me this way. But I was relieved and said it was no big deal.

As the plane headed toward Connecticut from Plano,

I realized no one would be happy for me, for us. No one would support this marriage. No one but his family. His parents loved me and so did Pete. Soon after Gabe and I got together, his parents warned me to not get too close because he didn't last very long outside prison and he always managed to find trouble. But as the months passed and he was still doing well they realized I was a good influence on him and I was keeping him safe. Well, as safe as I could.

My heart sank as I thought about telling my sister Sophie. I would see the disapproval on her face and I could already hear it in her voice. But she would support me because she loved me, I thought. My mind was now all over the place and by the time my flight landed safely in Connecticut, I decided it was my life and I would say yes to him if I wanted to. But did I?

Seeing Gabe at the airport waiting for me always gave me a jolt. Seeing his tanned face and those green eyes scanning for me always made me feel loved. Before he said his first word to me, he was anyone I wanted him to be. Walking toward him, in my mind, he was perfect. Accepting. Trusting. But then we said hello and he questioned why I was wearing a tissue T-shirt or why my jeans hung low, I was snapped back into reality. It was only in my mind that he was who I wanted him to be. He grabbed my hand, my bag, and led the way with me trying to catch up to his quicker pace. But I was used to this. I knew it wasn't right, but again, I stayed.

I still wasn't sure this would be the weekend he proposed, but as we pulled up to his parents' house and I saw the size of the smiles on his parents' faces, I was beginning to think it was. I felt hopeful yet disgusted. For most of the relationship to that point that's how I felt. I loved him but I hated how he treated me. But I was always convinced that I could change him. That I could love the bad out of him. So I stayed, always hoping for the best.

The weekend progressed. We had dinner with his parents and I visited some of my friends. The next day we headed from Cheshire to Maine, a six-hour car ride. We planned to spend the night there and the next day to see his family for brunch.

The drive to Maine was a familiar one, and it dug up a memory from 1994 that was comfortably resting under a pile of dust in the back of my mind. When Derek and

I were together we made the same trip around the same time of year. Derek and I checked into a hotel across the street from the beach. I was three months' pregnant, but we had never spent the night together. We hardly knew each other. As he unpacked I went outside on the balcony and took in the view. Behind the sounds of the cars buzzing by I could hear the ocean crashing into the shore and kids squealing with delight. The smells of pizza and freshly made ice cream cones filled my nostrils and made me nauseous.

While I was standing outside with the wind slightly against my face and the sun warming it, Derek came out and stood next to me. He told me he loved me and our unborn baby. He told me he wanted to make a good life together and that he would do what he had to make that possible. He followed that up by getting down on one knee, handing me a ring, and asking me to marry him. I was shocked. I had no idea what to say. Eventually he nudged me along by saying "well?" And with tear-soaked eyes and shock on my face, I said yes. He scooped me up and hugged me.

That memory flooded my mind as Gabe and I made

our way down the same highway, headed in the same direction. I took that memory and tucked it away. It was time to make new memories, with someone new. I looked over at Gabe and he looked back at me with that perfect smile and those green eyes I loved so much and I nestled my hand into his, squeezed it a little tighter, and let him lead the way on that stormy, late-afternoon day in April.

As we reached the hotel and found a place to park, Gabe hopped out with an extra pep in his step and led us to the front desk area. We checked in, handed over our bags to the bellhop and followed him to our room. After settling in, Gabe had to leave for a few minutes and then returned happier than he was before he left. This entire weekend so far was great. He was in a good mood and things were going well between us. At times when I thought he would be upset, he wasn't. I started to relax a little more with him.

We sat outside on the balcony taking in the ocean view and just sitting close together until the weather turned for the worse and a thunderstorm rolled in. The waves hit the rocks hard and lightning was getting closer. We made our way inside and got ready for dinner. He had made a reservation for dinner downstairs at the hotel restaurant. I wondered if tonight was the night. I wondered when it was coming. I got ready and put on my size-twelve interview outfit and together we walked downstairs to the restaurant.

Our table was near the floor-to-ceiling window. I loved sitting close to the water and with the storm, the waves were massive. As they crashed against the rock you could hear them explode. When the lightning struck it illuminated the ocean and the view was a show. He and I sat close and ordered drinks. I figured if the proposal was coming and it was going to be public, I needed some liquid courage to say yes. Part of me was dreading it and hoping he would not do it, but another part of me, the romantic, co-dependent part of me, wanted him to.

Drinks came and went and so did dinner. We laughed and reminisced. We had a great time enjoying each other. For the first time in a very long time I was not on eggshells. I was not afraid of him exploding like the waves. I was relaxed and I was happy. Gabe was back. The original Gabe I had fallen in love with. He was back and he was here with me again and I didn't want to let him go. This

Gabe was the Gabe I wanted to marry and spend the rest of my life with. The Gabe I wanted to take care of. The Gabe I wanted to sleep with forever.

The bill came just after dessert was finished and my heart raced and felt sad at the same time. As we got up and left the restaurant, I thought to myself well, maybe he'll do it tomorrow. I honestly felt disappointed. In the elevator we stood close to each other and made small talk with the people riding with us. Gabe, holding my hand and then placing his arm around me and pulling me in closer, didn't seem to care that I was dressed like a substitute teacher in size-twelve clothes. He presented as proud to be with me and I fell a little closer into him.

Both a little drunk and with me now over the fact that tonight was not the night, we stumbled into our room. He undressed and put on a tank top that I hated. I made fun of it as I slipped on my sweats and washed the day off my face. Minutes after brushing my teeth, I hopped on the bed and Gabe went out on the deck. When he came back in he had a dozen red long-stem roses wrapped with an exquisite red ribbon. They were beautiful. He walked over to me, got down on one knee and handed me the roses. I was in shock. I didn't expect him to do this on this night and in that shirt. But his familiar green eyes were full of tears and as he opened a little white box with a beautiful yet familiar ring inside and with tears running down his face, he asked me to marry him.

I looked up at him and without hesitation, I said yes and I threw my arms around him. He stood up, threw me on the bed and kissed me, passionately. A few seconds later he opened the champagne he had and we toasted to us. As we laid in the bed and listened to the rain, we talked in the dark. He held my hand, rubbed his thumb on mine and I felt safe. Happy. I had Gabe back and we were getting married.

Minutes later as the rain continued to fall and his snoring began, I lay awake with everything rushing through my mind. How were we going to tell people? Would I be supported? Would the mean Gabe come back? Yes. Yes he would. I knew he would resurface. He always did. But tonight he was nowhere to be found. I loved the happier version of Gabe and he was the one here with me tonight. I closed my eyes and tried to sleep. I held onto to him tight. It was a mixture of his snoring and the weather that rocked my heavy mind to sleep that night.

The next morning the storm had cleared and the day was sunny and new. We got up, packed up, and headed back to Cheshire. We stopped for muffins and picked up a few for the ride back. But before leaving Maine, we hit up a restaurant for a quick breakfast. With a shiny new ring on my left hand that fit perfectly, we made our way inside. We were seated right away outside on the patio facing the ocean. He pulled out my chair and I sat down. The waitress came over and we ordered drinks. As the drinks came and bread made itself at home on the table, we toasted us again and looked out at the view.

I have no idea how he was feeling. I would come to realize I never knew how he was feeling. Even if he was emotional I could never tell if his feelings were real or true, but as for me I knew how I was feeling in that moment. I knew this version of Gabe would soon be leaving and the real one would be back. The reality of being engaged to him was going to soon set in. I figured I would enjoy him and this feeling as long as it lasted. I knew that the moment we left Maine, the real Gabe would creep in and it would feel as if it had been a dream.

Looking at him staring out at the water I could see the good in him. The innocence of him. His heart was there and it was big. Although it was covered in jealousy, insecurity, and dishonesty, it was there nonetheless. That is what I wanted to uncover. I wanted to dismantle all of his bad and reveal all of his good. As I studied the lines on his face and saw his motion to pick up his drink, I picked up my drink, adjusted my sunglasses, sat back in my chair and with a smile on my face I told Gabe how much I loved him and how happy I was. In that moment I felt safe, secure, happy, and hopeful. I didn't want to leave that restaurant. I knew once I left I would be leaving him there as well and I loved him with all my heart.

After leaving the restaurant, we had plans to meet Gabe's family in Cheshire for a late lunch. We hopped in the car and as we did I felt sick. I knew we were leaving and I didn't want to. I wanted to stay in our own little bubble where no one knew me. No one knew him. No one knew us. I liked the idea of people viewing us as a happy couple who were newly engaged and not a couple of idiots struggling, constantly fighting and tearing each other down. But we drove towards Cheshire and into our certain demise.

At the restaurant his family was waiting for us. His mom, Patricia, his dad, Gabe Sr., Pete, his wife Samantha, and of course their two kids. When we walked in they were already seated. When they saw us walk in they all got up, rushed us both and greeted us with glowing hugs and a few cards congratulating us. His mom and his sister-in-law jumped at the opportunity to look at the ring and they pulled me away asking how he proposed. They, unlike the men, wanted to know every juicy detail.

I told the story as best I could and the smile splashed across my face was real. The love I felt in that moment was real. Heavy. Missed. We, in that moment, were both surrounded with love from a family, a feeling Gabe knew, but a feeling I was not so familiar with. Gabe and I sat close together after his family was satisfied with the ring viewing and a romantic story we would share for a long time to come. I felt warm inside, safe, and secure. A part of me knew I was going to miss those moments from that day because I knew they were not going to last but the other part of me, the bigger part of me that day, pushed out those fears and just enjoyed the warmth of a loving family and the hope for a positive future.

After the late lunch, we all got into separate cars and went in different directions. But not before big hugs and kisses were handed out by his mom and dad and a loud cheerful "welcome to the family" was shouted in my direction. Hearing that made me happy. I had not known the love of a family until I met his family. Pete right away was the annoying older brother. His mom slid comfortably in the role of mom and since my dad had passed, his dad filled that role for me, including scolding me for "useless purchases." He would roll his eyes and walk out of the room. Little did he know how happy he made my heart. I was not only in love with Gabe, but his family as well.

A day later it was time for me to head back to Texas. It was time for me to tell my friends and my family I was engaged to Gabe. This is when I feared the trouble was going to begin and I wasn't wrong. Gabe dropped me off at the airport and with a heavy heart and mind I walked away from him. I needed some time alone to think and figure things out. I had some decisions to make.

I walked through security with my shoes, belt, and watch Derek had given me for our tenth anniversary all off. I collected my things, found my gate, made myself comfortable, and called Derek. He answered my call in two rings, per usual. He asked me if I were okay and I let him think I was. We made small talk and then I blurted it out. I told him Gabe asked me to marry him and he asked me what I said. I told him I said yes and he said congratulations. Then he asked me what was wrong. For the next thirty minutes while I looked at my new ring, I told Derek about my fears. I explained to him what I feeling and how hard it was with Gabe. Derek listened and after I finished pouring my heart to him, he told me only I knew what was best for me and that he would support any decision I made. I thanked him and we hung up. As they called my flight number to board I texted Gabe that I loved him and I powered down my phone.

Chapter Nine

I have always hated the Yankee Swap, that gift exchange where anyone can take a gift away from anyone else. Well, I guess it's unfair to say always. I have hated it since the second grade. Since Shirley Hellman, all blonde, showered, and put together, walked over to me with her lame gift pick and took my gift.

I remember having my turn during our second grade Christmas party. Our desks were in a U-shape. We all picked our numbers and the Yankee Swap began. I remember looking at the gift piles in the middle of the room.

The night before, I'd asked my mom to get something for me so I could participate in the swap. She did. I grabbed up the plastic tube she handed to me holding colorful bracelets, earrings, and hair ties. I remember thinking, "I am so glad this is not my gift."

I was a total tomboy. I am not sure if I was a tomboy because I wanted to be alone or by default. I had four brothers and one sister. My brothers had freedoms my sister and I did not have. They could cross the street.

Run in the sprinkler without their shirts on and stay up late. My sister and I wanted the same freedoms, so we did the same things. One day in early fall of the same year as second grade, while at the store with my mom, the cashier referred to me as her son. I was so proud. Mission accomplished, I thought.

So while I wrapped up the over-the-top girly gift my mom supplied, I was excited at the thought of the next day and fantasized about what I would get from the Yankee Swap. Christmas in my house was not a fun holiday. Not many of the holidays in my house were fun.

If I had to say which one was my favorite, I would say Valentine's Day. Valentine's Day was the only "holiday" in my house where my dad was not drunk, passed out on the floor, or screaming at us. He saved that behavior for Christmas, Thanksgiving, and Easter. But Valentine's Day was his holiday for us, his kids. Each year when we woke up on February 14th we anticipated a special Valentine from dad. Just dad. Not mom. This was a day my dad chose to tell us he loved us. Never with words, but with cards and candy.

The doorbell would ring and the delivery man

would be at the door with two long boxes holding long-stem roses, one for me and the other for my sister. It was a custom he did each year. Without fail.

My parents didn't have a lot of money. My dad had his vices and those vices were front and center as a reminder each holiday. They showed up under the tree each year where gifts from Santa were supposed to be. My parents did the best they could, but as kid I was hopeful. I was hopeful when I believed in Santa. On Christmas Eve I would put my little hands together, squeeze my eyes tight and pray that I would get what I had asked for. Each year I would be disappointed. There was something the under the tree—never what I wanted—but there was something.

So on the eve of the Yankee Swap and the signal that we were about to have a few weeks off from school, I was excited at the thought of maybe getting something cool. I wrapped my little gift and went to bed.

That day I went to school in the usual way, with an empty stomach, grime on my hands, and torn-up clothes, but a pep in my step. I got to my classroom and placed my gift in the pile with all of the other ones. As I did I surveyed the other brightly wrapped packages and tried to decide which one I would choose first if I was lucky enough to get the first pick. As the day progressed, we took our spelling test, studied math, picked verbs out of sentences and had recess. The clock was ticking down to party time. And finally, after hours of waiting it was time.

The numbers were picked out of a hat and we all sat at our desks with half-eaten cookies and candy canes on our little plates. As each kid got up and picked out a package, it was closer and closer to being my turn. But as I sat there I noticed my awkwardly wrapped package was still in the center of the room.

My turn came and I picked a gift. When all was said and done, everyone had an unopened gift. At the teacher's say-so we unwrapped and then the swapping would begin. I was so excited to see my gift.

My mom and my siblings were amazing artists. My mom has this amazing ability to bring drawings to life. She has such talents I had no idea why she did not paint or draw more. She handed down her ability and her talents to my siblings. My brother Brian received most of her talents but the others received their fair share as well. Me, not so much, and my mom made sure I knew I could not draw. I am not someone you want on your Pictionary team.

So when I unwrapped my Yankee Swap gift I was over the moon to see colored pencils, crayons, tracing paper and an instruction booklet on how to draw. I remember thinking that if I could draw maybe my mom would pay more attention to me. Maybe she would accept me in the same way she accepted the others. I looked up and no one noticed my cool gift. No one would swap it.

In elementary school I wasn't popular. I didn't have many friends in my class. The lack of money my parents had showed on my dirty skin, unwashed hair and by the hand-me-downs I had from my brothers. So no one paid much attention to me.

Until Shirley Hellman saw what I had and decided she wanted it. She walked toward me with her friends. She was holding the gift of plastic bracelets, hair ties, and earrings I had wrapped the night before. I pleaded with her to let me keep the drawing kit, but her friend yelled at me that she could take what she wanted, and she did.

I went home that day after school and as I sat on the bus looking out the window, I held my own gift. A gift I didn't want. The sadness that I would never learn how to draw and earn my mom's love set in. I sank down on the green pleather seat next to no one and closed my eyes.

Fast forward to one year later, the third grade. It was during my time in the third grade that I realized who I was. I realized what I meant to do on this earth. How I would leave my mark. Which direction my life needed to go in. But it wasn't until thirty years later that I could comfortably leave my mark.

I found out a week before I began the third grade that my teacher was going to be Mrs. Franklin. I was excited to be in her class because my older brother Brian also had her and she seemed nice. The year progressed. I turned nine that October and as Thanksgiving approached, so did the holidays.

As we prepared for the holiday Mrs. Franklin handed out a writing assignment. She handed each kid in the class a greeting card. As she walked around the room handing them out randomly, she explained to the class that we were to look at our greeting cards, study them, and describe in an essay what we saw. We were to be creative because this was a test grade. As she passed my desk she handed me my card. I looked at it and liked what I saw.

Mine was a Christmas card. There were animal decorations hanging from a tree branch and the animals were wearing little Christmas hats and holding candy canes. Without thinking or stressing, I began to write.

What poured out of me that day was the beginning of me. I easily described what was on my card. I gave them names, jobs, and had them in conversations with each other. To me, this was easy. I wanted each assessment to be this easy. I had no idea if what I had done was good or not, but I happily handed in my essay and opened my dreaded math book. I hated math. I still hate math.

A few days later my teacher told me she had called my mom so they could discuss my essay. I looked at her while her words came at me like daggers. My little stomach dropped and I wanted to poop. I had no idea why my mom was coming in, but I knew I didn't like the idea. I went back to my desk and put my head down. When the recess bell rang all the kids left, except me. I waited in my dirty clothes for my mother.

I lifted my head when Mrs. Franklin said my mom was there. We all sat down at the community table and my mom shot me a look. A "why am I here look," and again I wanted to poop. Mrs. Franklin pulled out my essay and the greeting card I wrote about. She read it out loud and as she did she had a smile across her face and she laughed.

As she finished she looked at my mom and she said, "Kelly is an amazing writer. She's going to be a writer when she grows up."

My face lit up. I did a good job. She went on to say how great my essay was and she asked me if she could keep it to show the other students what a good essay looks like. I looked over at my mom, knowing she was going to wrap me up in her arms and tell me how proud she was of me. But instead when I looked at her, she had a scowl on her face. She asked my teacher if that was the only reason she was asked to be at the school. My teacher had a blank look on her face and my mom looked at me and said, "Writing is not an art form," and left. I was crushed.

From my earliest memories of my mom, she was the best. I have so many great memories of her. When I was five, I remember her making me the most unbelievable Barbie doll birthday cake. I can still see her in all of her blonde, silky hair glory. She stood tall and proud in her fluffy, delicious, pink frosting gown and was completely amazing. I loved it. As I scooped that first sweet delicious bite into my mouth I stared at Barbie and thought, "I wish I had her hair."

My mom loved to bake, a master baker in my eyes, especially around Christmas. I remember as a kid, my siblings and I would help my mom make homemade caramels. We'd wrap them up in wax paper and stuff them in jars for Christmas gifts for the extended family. We had so much fun wrapping the ends in the wax paper to look like real candy. We'd laugh, talk, listen to Christmas music, and I am pretty sure we ate more than we wrapped. I also remember her cookie press shooting out Christmas-shaped butter cookies. She was an artist with that thing and I always wanted to use it, but wasn't old enough. I would watch her as she worked and wonder how I had gotten so lucky to have a mother like her.

Early on my mom seemed to know about everything. She always knew where our shoes were or what we were having for dinner. She always knew where all of us were, and that was not easy, considering there was six of us. And she kept us safe. There was a period where a man dressed as a clown was driving around our neighborhood trying to lure kids to his creepy red, windowless van. But she kept us in, kept tabs on us, until he was caught.

I remember sitting around listening to her funny stories. She could always make us laugh. As a family, we didn't have much, but boy could we laugh. Out of the six of us kids, three of us got my mom's sense of humor and I was one of the lucky three. I am the spitting image of my mom, from my looks to my personality. Sometimes when I laugh I can hear her instead of me. I wanted to be just like her when I grew up. When someone told me we looked alike my face lit up, and why wouldn't it? She was my mom. She was the greatest! The one thing I got from my dad was his ears. I have no idea where my hair came from except maybe hell. The color fits.

Thinking about her now and how I want to remember her, before things got dark, I can still see my mom with a smile on her face. I can still smell the Cover Girl foundation she used to wear. I loved to sit and watch her put on her makeup and brush her hair. She had shoulder-length, wavy blonde hair that was always styled and brushed and makeup that was always perfect. I still remember her checked dress coat that she would wear over her brown ribbed turtleneck sweater to create a fashionable ensemble. She looked so put-together, happy and confident. She'd walk in a room, gleaming with confidence, looking as if she just dominated a boardroom, took it over, kicked ass and took names.

For me, her presence would make the room shine brighter. She could make anything fun by just laughing; that magical, contagious laugh that I can still hear sometimes. She could turn the hardest of times into good times with that powerful smile. She could take attention away from my drunken dad just by putting on music, dancing around the room, telling jokes and laughing. If she laughed, you knew something was truly funny. And the greatest feeling was when she would laugh at my sarcastic remarks. So much of who I am came from my mom. My personality, my toughness, my sense of humor, my survival skills, my ability to persevere, and my feet, were gifts from my mother.

But then something changed. I am not sure what happened to her, but one day the darkness came. It set in. Loomed. She no longer smiled, she didn't laugh as much, and laundry didn't get done. She got angry and yelled. That confident woman who owned the boardroom left and never came home. She stopped taking care of herself. Dinners went unmade. Laundry piled up. And dad and his demons disappeared for days on end. I am not sure if something specific happened but whatever it was, it changed everything. Something took over her emotions that caused her to abandon her children emotionally. I know my mom loved us, but something made her stop showing it. I think that thing was called life.

As a child, I mistook her depression and unhappiness for her not liking me. Of course, looking back, I can try to tell myself it was depression, not me. But feeling that your own mother doesn't love you is a pretty hard thing to live with. The problem was that she checked out at the time I really needed her to check in. She never helped me with my hair or makeup, or with any of my boy questions. I was conditioned not to ask questions of her on these matters starting at an early age.

When I was eight I asked her what a period was. Her advice was that when I pissed blood I should let her know. I didn't start my period until I was thirteen. So for the next five years, I was terrified every time I went to the bathroom. One day on the bus headed home from school, I heard someone say a word I had never heard before, but I knew it was something bad. I came home and asked my mother, "What's a cunt?" Her eyes grew large and her face got red and she slapped me hard across the face. "Don't you ever say that disgusting word again!" I was crying, startled, and in physical pain, but I still didn't know what that word meant. It was like a cloud of doom hung over our house and every time I came home, I waited for that clap of thunder.

I can't imagine how hard it was for her raising six kids, basically alone, with an alcoholic husband. But after a day with her unkempt, angry self, all my dad had to do was walk through the door to look like a superstar. Even if he was drunk, he still came home and played with us. In our eyes he was a hero. For her, I am sure it destroyed her even more.

We didn't have a lot of money because of my dad's demons, so she only went to the store about once every two weeks. That caused some of us to hoard food. Sophia and I would take canned goods, like SpaghettiOs, and hide them in our room. John always went for the cereal. Days later, after all the food was gone, John would come out of nowhere with a box of cereal. When we tried to have some, he yelled at us and insisted it was only his. We didn't ever have shampoo, soap, toothpaste or laundry detergent. The years of my life from about ten to until I moved out, I don't remember a day that I wasn't dealing with adult problems. I don't remember a day that I wasn't hungry, my teeth didn't hurt or I wasn't worried about whether we had electricity or heat.

When I was twelve, I got a job at Dunkin' Donuts. I can't remember how I was able to do that being that I was so young, except that my friend's parents owned it so they gave me a job. From the start, I had to give up my tips to my dad, and every other paycheck went to the house bills. My dad spent my tips on milk, cigarettes, gas; whatever he needed. I spent the rest of my paycheck on things for me; toiletries or clothes. But whenever I did, my siblings would use them. I was able to eat there so that was good. All of my siblings worked at food establishments, so we never starved. We had just had to learn to be creative at finding food.

On our days off, we often would go to a friend's house where we knew we could eat. I loved to go to Julia's house. And every Sunday, we went to my grandmother's house for dinner. No one ever came to our house, mostly because my dad was so miserable to be around, so my grandmother didn't know how bad things were, and we never told her. In fact there was nothing to tell, because we were so used to living that way it wasn't unusual for us. But I always felt she didn't like me. I knew she loved me, by default, but she didn't like me. I always felt as if I was a burden to her.

After my writing discovery, all I wanted to do was write. So I did. Words easily flowed from my mind to my hands and then splashed onto paper. My mind was always busy, always cluttered. I realized my brain had always been that way, and now I knew why. I was an exposed nerve. I felt everything. I felt everything I was feeling, everything my dog was feeling and everything anyone around me was feeling. But I had no idea how to express this. Until I learned to write. I wrote in my room. When my mom came in I hid whatever I was writing. She hated it. She felt an art form was painting or drawing. But for me writing was what I wanted to do. What I needed to do.

I had a notebook with every page full of short stories, poems, and feelings. I kept it hidden in my closet in my bedroom. At night after my sister fell asleep, I got it out and by the light of our nightlight, I wrote. I wrote for hours. I didn't want anyone to know what I was doing for fear of my mom finding out that I was writing. When she did find out, it was not fun for me.

One afternoon I was sitting in my room. I heard her and my older brother laughing. Moments later they were both standing in my doorway holding a familiar piece of paper. I looked up at her and without saying anything she began to read out loud what I had written down. It was a poem I had written and thought I hid. As she read she sounded out the words I had misspelled. She and my brother laughed at me, my poor spelling, and my words. My words, at times, were all I had. My words made me happy and I loved them. I found comfort in them. After she made fun of me, she crumpled up the paper and threw it on the floor. They walked away and I was left alone on my bed feeling stupid. I didn't write for a while after that. I was scared. I was embarrassed. I was alone.

I wish I could sit here and look back on this time in my young life and say my mom snapped out of it and accepted that I loved to write. Accepted that I am who I am and that I did not have to hide in plain sight, but I can't. As I grew things just seemed to get worse. I could see that my dad's demons were killing her and I hated that. I hated seeing my mom so miserable. She would sit in her bedroom with the door shut and the shades down. She would stay in there for hours in the dark, smoking and sleeping. I would try to check on her but either she was asleep or said she wanted to be left alone.

Although we never had a healthy mother-daughter relationship I still loved her. She was, after all, my mom. So I tried to help her. On the days she seemed down I would buy her a card to let her know that I loved her. I would leave it for her on her bed. Other times I got her a stuffed animal or a balloon. I would bring home her favorite donuts from work or bags of coffee to let her know she was appreciated and that I was thinking about her.

But she never acknowledged the things I did for her. It was almost as if it was expected. Which was confusing to me because out of the six of us, I was the only one doing anything like that. But I figured if I continued doing these things, she would notice and she would love me.

One afternoon during a school break from high school while I was working two jobs, I got home from my first job to change for my second job. I walked into my house; no one was home. Nothing unusual. I looked in the fridge and it was empty. I placed my hand across my stomach as it growled, shut the fridge door, and figured I would eat during my second job. I walked upstairs to get into my uniform and as I opened my bedroom door I noticed a pile of something on my bed. As I walked closer to inspect what it was, my stomach took a turn. It went from hunger to dropping when I realized what I was looking at.

Every card, every stuffed animal, every balloon on a stick I had given my mom was torn to bits and shredded and left for me on my bed. Staring up at me as if to say I never mattered. My heart, at sixteen, was broken in the same way it was when I was nine. I was lost and confused. I had been showing her how much I loved her and how much I cared. I was working two jobs to help with the bills and this is what she does to me? I was broken.

I scooped everything up and put it in the trunk in

front of my bed. I placed it next to my hidden notebooks full of my feelings, short stories, and poems. I changed into my uniform and with a head full of confusion and a heavy heart, I left my house to serve donuts and coffee.

Looking back on it today, begging and chasing for love and attention was all I knew. I was taught at an early age that I was not good enough to be naturally loved. If your mom does not love you, who will? We seem to be drawn to what we know, what we are used to. For me, I was used to begging for love, although I had no clue that was what I was doing. Because things at home or with my mom were always off, I had no idea what it felt like when things were good. If I had a friend treat me well, I shied away from that because it felt odd to me, but when someone treated me poorly, I was attracted to it like a bug to a light. Even if I got zapped, it still felt normal to me so it's what I looked for in relationships. When Gabe began to treat me poorly, that was when I got most comfortable. That's when it felt most like home.

Chapter Ten

April 2013

I was at my house. The house my three sons and I moved into after their dad and I divorced. The house was a split-level. Upstairs was the oversized living room with floor-to-ceiling windows; up a few steps was the bar area leading into the dining room. A set of French doors led to the back deck holding the grill and fire pit. Through another door off the dining room and a few steps down was the kitchen, making an appearance straight from the '80s. Around the corner sat the master bedroom. Downstairs was a large living area and two bedrooms. My oldest son has his room while the younger two shared. While the kids and I were home and my ex-husband's parents were visiting, my doorbell rang. Confused, I looked at my kids and went to the door.

Two women were at the door. As I looked them both over with many thoughts racing through my head, I saw that one had a smile splattered across her face, short brown hair, and was on the heavier side. While the other one, the one that looked as if she were in charge, lacked a smile, had short black hair, and looked as if she were in running shape. But it was her friendly eyes that somehow put me at ease even after noticing the gun placed neatly on her hip. As I looked at the gun, the FBI logo on her blue jacket screamed for me to notice it, and I did.

After a short few seconds we had a brief intro and I was informed they wanted to discuss my then-boyfriend Gabe. As I let them in, leading them downstairs, I sent my young sons back upstairs to their grandparents. I told all of them, in a shaky voice with a sudden case of dry mouth, that the women were there to help me redecorate the house. The kids ran for cover at the sound of anything girly and left us alone to quietly have a private conversation.

I walked them to the lower level of the house. Sandra sat on the couch, I took the seat next to her, and Barbara sat close to us in the freestanding chair. They introduced Sandra as Gabe's potential parole officer and Barbara as her partner. Sandra asked me if I knew why she was there and I told her I knew. I told her I had spoken to Steve, Gabe's parole officer back in Connecticut, and he told me they were coming by to talk to me about Gabe moving to

Texas.

After a few minutes of small talk, Barbara being the friendlier of the two, we got down to business. Sandra asked me if I knew who Gabe was. She wanted to know if I knew about his record and his violent past. I did, I told her. I knew about his jail time. I knew about the drug deals and I knew about his friend setting him up.

But then she asked me if I knew about the domestic violence arrests in his file. I sat back and got lost in memories of Gabe telling me how awful his ex-girlfriends were to him. How they upset him and how he did get violent. I thought about the ex he stuffed in his trunk and tried to drown shortly after driving her to the river because she was talking to another guy. I flashed back to the way he spoke to his mom. How he called her names and put her down because her kitchen was a mess. While he cussed her out I stood there and thought to myself, "He would never talk to me like that." I recalled the story he told me of how she upset him to the point that he wrapped the telephone cord around her neck and tried to strangle her. And the time he knocked over his dad who was sitting on his recliner and choked him out because Gabe could not control his anger.

I snapped out of it and looked at Sandra. My heart was racing, because I knew if I messed this up for Gabe he would be upset. I thought carefully about each word before it came out of my mouth. I told her I knew about all of it. She then looked at me as if to say, "Are you fucking serious." Then without notice, she slammed a file on my lap. A file that was thick. Heavy. Papers sticking out because there was not much room left for them. It had to have weighted at least three pounds. I looked at her and asked what this was.

"This is Gabe's rap sheet," she said boldly. Annoyed. Trying to get her point across.

"Is this who you want in your life? Is this the kind of man you want around your kids? A man who hits women? A criminal?" She stared at me with her meaningful eyes, trying to convince me this was a bad idea without actually saying it.

I looked away and sat with a heavy mind. I remembered what Steve said one afternoon when we spoke on the phone.

"You seem like a smart girl. You have a big heart.

What the hell are you doing with him? He is dangerous. You need to walk away. Think before you get him further into your life. He does not take any of this seriously and you deserve better."

I looked at Barbara and she offered nothing. "But," I thought to myself, "he is not this guy anymore. He loves me. He would never hit me. He would never do anything to hurt my kids. He's much better now. He's changed."

Seeing that I was not getting it, Sandra opened the file. She showed me his mug shots. Wow, he had told me whenever he got arrested he smiled because he didn't give a fuck and he was so proud of that. He would tell me stories of the cops chasing him and him getting away. He would brag about getting into fights with FBI agents and breaking their bones. But when I looked at his mug shots, he was not smiling. He was overweight. Sad. Miserable.

I took a breath and thought to myself, if he was lying about smiling in his mug shots, what else was he lying about? I didn't want to know. I didn't want to face that maybe he was not who he said he was, so I buried my questions deep in a dark place and covered them with good memories of him so I would never know, but those mug shots popped into my head almost every day after seeing them. I knew Sandra was right. I knew he was probably not someone I should have had in my life.

With Sandra and Barbara in my house, as I sat on my couch holding Gabe's rap sheet, I found myself in the middle of another dark memory. A few months before the FBI darkened my doorstep, I was back home visiting Gabe. It was a usual visit in the sense of departure, arrival, and being picked up at the airport. I arrived late at night. Gabe was there waiting for me at the baggage claim complete with that smile, those green eyes, and his cologne so thick in the air that I could smell him before I could see him. As we walked to his car, hand in hand with a little more pep in our step because of the cold winter night, I saw my bottle of water and a surprise addition, cheesecake. We'd recently had a conversation about cheesecake from a place in Hartford, and before picking me up he stopped by and picked up a slice for me. I thought it was so sweet of him to think of me this way.

On the ride back to his place, I fed him cheesecake as he drove and we caught up. We laughed and I rubbed his neck as he took me to his apartment just like usual. He looked over at me with those green eyes and I felt happy and safe. He was happy and for me in that moment that was all that mattered. We got to his place and went to bed.

The next morning he got ready for work and I drove him in. I would drive him and pick him up so I didn't need to rent a car. But on this morning, like any day with him, I had no idea what would set him off. As I approached the highway I usually took to get to his gym, he suddenly wanted me to take another route, and when I swerved to go in another direction, the tire hit the side of the road. Gabe was pissed. He started to yell at me. Call me names. My stomach began to rot. Tears filled up and poured down my face. My body was hot but I was frozen. He continued to call me names and then stopped talking to me altogether.

I dropped him off and I knew I needed to get out of this relationship. Things started to build with him but he had a way with words. With trickery. We went out to a party one night around the holidays. He was off chatting with someone so I was at the bar talking to one of his friends. He saw me take a sip from his friend's drink. He came over, grabbed me by the arm and said we were leaving. He pulled me along and as we were leaving he saw people he knew. We would stop, and as he sung my praises to his friends, his grip got tighter. As we edged closer to the door I was thinking maybe he was not mad at me anymore. He had just told someone how lucky he was that someone like me even gave him the time of day.

I let my breath go and we made our way to the car. He opened the door and I thought for sure I was in the clear. Nope. Not even close. He got in the car and then ripped into me. I was a filthy whore for embarrassing him in front of everyone the way I did. How could I sip another man's drink? How could I do that to him? I was stunned. Confused. I had no idea what to say to him. How to calm him down. When I tried to defend myself, it just made him even more upset.

A few miles later, I was on the side of the road in the dead of winter in Hartford. He'd kicked me out of the car. This is how the relationship was. He was sweet and kind and the next minute he was a tornado full of hatred, acting if he could not care less about me and trying to hurt me in any way that he could.

I was kicked out of the car a few other times too. I

started to just accept that this was who I loved and this was who he was. Soon enough, it all became just normal. The tight chest. The eggshells. I became comfortable in the dark with my mouth shut and not much of a say-so in anything unless he asked for my opinion.

But I was finally starting to see it, to feel it. I started to wonder why I accepted this behavior. Slowly my friends were fading. No one called me anymore. They were sick of hearing how awful Gabe was one minute and then about how great he was the next minute. I would cry and laugh. I was questioned about why I was with him and when someone told me how awful he treated me, I would get upset. I stayed because of fear. At first I thought maybe my friends and then my sister and eventually my brother were just not supportive. At first I thought they didn't want me happy. But when I began to find myself completely alone with just Gabe, I knew something had to change, but I was not ready to change just yet. I was not ready to give up on him. To give up on us.

Sometimes I called Derek and shared things with him. During one call he asked "What happened to the Kelly I know? The Kelly who would not take shit from anyone? Why are you taking it from him?" I think it is because I was so mean to Derek that I was afraid of being mean to Gabe. I have no medium. No balance. Either I was a raging bitch, or I was a doormat. And for now, with Gabe, I was a doormat.

After I got back from dropping Gabe off at work that day, the day he yelled at me and called me names for hitting the tire against the curb, my cell phone rang. I looked at the caller ID and it was Allen, Derek's best friend and Todd's godfather. I have known Alan for sixteen-plus years. He grew up in the house next door to Derek. Allen was with me during my pregnancy with Todd. Derek was away in college and could not be near me, so Allen picked up where Derek left off. He was with me for the ultrasound, Lamaze class and eventually during labor. We had a good relationship and I loved him like a brother. Any time I needed help, Allen was there for me. More than Derek ever was. Even after the divorce, Allen was supportive. Checking on me and the kids.

So when I looked down and saw it was Allen calling, I felt it was a sign. I answered. I told him I needed help and within minutes he was at Gabe's house helping me pack up my stuff and getting out of there. As we got in his car he asked me if I was pregnant. I laughed.

"No," I said, "I'm just an idiot."

Soon after we left, Gabe started to call me. He left me a few messages, but when he didn't hear back, he blew up my phone. After we got to Allen's house he got me a ticket back to Plano. He set up a ride for me to get to the airport and then he was off to work. Like usual, Allen jumped in and saved me.

When the adrenaline of packing up and fleeing wore off, I called Pete, Gabe's brother. After talking to him, he agreed that the best thing for me would be for me to go home and forget Gabe. Move on with my life. In his words, Gabe was not worth all of this. Gabe was not worth the trouble and the mess. He said things would just get worse and that Gabe would take me down with him.

Instead of me paying attention to reality, I suddenly felt bad for Gabe. Was I just another person giving up on him? My plans then changed. I called my friend to come get me. I had Julia pick me up. We drove back to Gabe's and I unpacked as quickly as I could. I had to make it look like I never left. And I did. I washed my face, called Gabe, and things were back to normal.

Allen was not happy. But I "loved" Gabe. My "love" for him blurred my reality. My "love" for him put me in danger. My "love" for him took over my love for me and my kids. My kids needed a healthy, happy mom and they didn't have that. Things I didn't see or understand while Sandra flipped the pages through his criminal file. I had convinced myself that Gabe was a good guy. That he just loved differently. Harder. That he was just more intense. I knew he loved me, I just had to try harder to love him in the way he needed me to.

After talking to Sandra for a few hours that day at my house, I decided it was probably not a great idea for Gabe to move in with me right away like we had planned. He was going to move to Plano, live with me and start his new job. But I had second thoughts. I told Sandra that maybe he needed his own place for the first six months. She agreed, but not until making sure I was making the right decision. She again gave me a warning, and then we agreed that he would move to Plano and live on his own for six months.

I was not sure how I felt, but I wanted them to leave

because I knew my phone would have missed calls, voice messages, and texts wondering where I had been for the past few hours. As they collected their things and I walked them out, Sandra looked at me and said, "If things go badly, it will take just one call to remove him." She handed me her cell number and wished me luck. After I shut the door behind them, I had questions to answer from my kids and their grandparents. I explained very little to all of them.

I then picked up the phone and called Gabe. At first he was mad, and then when I explained to him who was at my house, he grew more and more upset. He was mad that they just showed up unannounced, he was mad that they had guns and he was mad that he didn't know about it beforehand. He then asked me how everything had gone. I tried to explain everything to him without mentioning the rap sheet, mug shot or the warnings.

A few weeks later we found out that his transfer was approved. I checked out, his job checked out, he had an apartment for six months and he was ready to go. He was still a prisoner of the State of Connecticut but he would be under the care of the State of Texas. He would have monthly check-ins and random drug testing.

He began to pack, gave away most of his stuff and quit his job in Connecticut. He was headed my way and I knew life was about to change but for me I was convinced that once we were a stable couple and no longer long-distance, things would get easier. I envisioned waking up together every Sunday. Having couple friends and maybe picking up a hobby together. I was looking forward to the kind of life I wanted with Derek but never had. I was looking forward to being with Gabe for the rest of my life. But was I wrong. I was dead wrong.

Gabe arrived in Texas in mid-August, just as my kids and I were moving into a new house. The one we had lived in after the divorce was too big and expensive, so I downsized. When Gabe rolled in, I had not yet finished moving in. The day he arrived was exciting. I was so happy he was with me. He showed up to the house wearing jeans and t-shirt and a 24-hour car ride. When I saw him I ran to him and hugged him. He came in and toured the house and then we lay down together on the mattress I had on the floor. We held each other and I fell into him. Safe. Secure. I had my plans for us nestled in my mind and my love for him on my sleeve.

As the days passed we managed to move everything in. Gabe, a control freak, made none of it easy. My sister and my brother-in-law came from San Antonio to help me. In front of them he was great, but he was easily annoyed. I was not super-organized so that made moving more difficult. He had no idea what I wanted to keep and what I didn't need. But at the end of the day I was finished moving out and we were in the same state.

He went to his apartment. He didn't have to do much with it because he wasn't planning on being there for very long, but he got dishes, bedding, and furniture anyway. Sandra was going by to check it out and to see how we were managing together.

We managed pretty well at first. He started his new job. Since he was a new trainer with no clients, he worked a lot. Late nights and early starts. I was trying to adjust to having a full-time boyfriend. When Gabe first moved to Plano I thought the relationship would be all-consuming, the way it was when I visited him, so when he wanted space to go out with the guys from work, I was upset. I didn't understand why he didn't want to come home to me, the way Derek did.

Between him working late and then going out after, I didn't see him much, but we were able to go out here and there and meet my friends. I was excited at the thought of Gabe meeting my friends. I wanted to integrate him into my circle. The idea of group dates, touring wineries, and maybe even weekend getaways was something I never had and I wanted to experience.

That December after Gabe moved here, one of my friends was hosting her annual "Christmas at the Hotel" holiday party. A handful of my really good friends were going and I was so excited to bring Gabe so he could meet everyone at once.

A few weeks before the party Gabe and I discussed the holidays. He was going to go home to see his family and I was going to stay in Plano to spend Christmas with my kids. Gabe said because he had just started working and didn't have a lot of money, we should skip gifts for each other and focus on my kids. I agreed. I am not the sort of person who needs gifts. If I want something I usually go buy it. But for our first Christmas, after Gabe mentioned that he wanted a watch, I gave him one. It wasn't the expensive, high-end one he'd said he wanted, but he loved it. He wore it all the time.

That year I decided I was going to upgrade him to something a little nicer. The day of my friend's party, I stopped by the jewelry store. I poked around until I found a watch that caught my eye. I walked out of the store with it gift wrapped and I was so excited to give it to him. My intention was to wait until Christmas, but the excited kid in me could not wait. As I drove to the gym to pick up Gabe, the gift wore a hole in my pocket. I picked him up and we made small talk. I told him who was going to be there and how I knew each person. I could not wait anymore. I told him I got him something and I wanted him to open it. As I drove I reached down and handed him the wrapped box.

At first he was upset. He said, "I said no gifts," but then I made him open it. As he ripped the paper off and opened the box, his face was priceless. He was speechless. I saw him gazing at the beautiful timepiece and then I watched tears drip down his face. He looked over at me and said, "No one has ever done anything like this for me before." He thanked me and put it on. That night we had fun. My friends liked him and he liked them as well. I felt we were off to a good start.

When we didn't have anywhere to go, we went to the movies or watched our TV shows. On nights when he worked late, I'd put on a show I recorded and rub his back for hours. Most of the time he fell asleep, but I was happy to just be there with him, and knowing I was able to relax him made me happy.

But when I called him during the day it would turn into a fight. It was as if he didn't want to be with me anymore. I would talk to his parents or my friends to figure out what was going on with him, but the more I asked the further away he got. He started coming home later and later and more intoxicated each night.

At times he didn't even come home. I would call him all night and wait up for him. I remember taking four sleeping pills so I could rest but even those didn't work. It was a constant fight. He would leave in the morning, I would tell him what I was making for dinner and I would ask him if he was coming home that night. He always said yes, but didn't. We fought. He would pack his stuff from my house and then bring it all back a few days later.

One day when he was at the house and in the shower,

I decided to look through his phone. He had changed the password. I knew something was off when he did that. He was hiding something. But what? I thought he was selling drugs again. My friends asked if maybe he was cheating. No way. I have never suspected him of cheating. Not on me. He left everything he knew in Connecticut to be with me, so why would he do that? The entire time we were together, even long distance, he'd never cheated. So that was off the table.

I was worried it was drugs or gambling. I didn't believe Gabe was like that until he was coming home drunk. One night after I had not seen much of him, he called asking me to meet up with him at work so we could go out. I got dressed as fast as I could and headed to see him. When I arrived at the gym, he had me follow him. He didn't say where we were going. Turns out we were going out with some of his friends. We met up at a house and went inside. Something had been off with Gabe lately. More than usual.

As we walked in he looked at me and said, "Didn't bother to do your hair?" He never said things like that to me. After walking in they started to drink. And then one by one they went into a back bedroom. He was headed there with a girl I didn't know. That upset me. When I asked what was going on, he admitted they were doing coke. That night was the first night Gabe hit me.

I stormed out of the house. I was so mad. He was on probation and subject to random drug testing. I was terrified he was going to go back to jail. I was angry and I was hurt. Had he been doing these things the entire time? Who was that girl? Is this where he was when he was not coming home?

He followed me outside. He yelled at me and I yelled back. He called me names and I did the same. I had no idea what I was doing there and I wanted to leave. He tried to stop me and I pushed him away.

Suddenly I didn't see Gabe, I saw a monster. He rushed over to me, grabbed my neck and lifted me off the ground. He told me to never touch him again. I tried to get his hand off of me but failed. He threw me down and walked back into the house.

I got in my car and drove away. I called him and told him he had to come home. Although he had just choked me, I was still worried about his random drug testing. I was still afraid he was going to go back to jail. He answered my call and I yelled at him and he told me to come back and get him. On the way back to my house I yelled at him and I was driving like a crazy person. I was so mad, so upset, and so scared. As I yelled and cried, I tore off the diamond necklace he had given me for Christmas when we first got together and I put it in the cup holder.

Things from there only got worse. He stopped communicating. Stopped coming home. His drinking was out of control. He was drinking right after work and then more at home, at least when he bothered to show up. On the nights I couldn't reach him, I got in my car and looked for him. The next day he always had an excuse. He had a meeting, or his friends wanted to go out with him. He said he didn't tell me when he wanted to go out because I would get mad at him, and he was not wrong.

A few weeks later he went back to Connecticut for Easter. I hardly heard from him. He ignored my calls and eventually I didn't hear from him until he was home. When he got back, he was hung over. He went to bed and then to work the next day.

Weeks later we had a fight. A massive fight. He said

things to me that he knew would set me off and they did. I got pissed and threw things at him and he did the same. He packed his stuff and yelled at me and I asked him if there was someone else. His response was, "I wish there was because that would hurt you and I want to hurt you." He then asked me for my engagement ring back and I refused to give it to him.

As he packed he raged. And then he was gone. My house was trashed. I was a wreck. I fell to the ground, crying. Confused. When will he be back? He usually took a few days, but this time was different. At the time I could not put my finger on it, but it was different and he was gone. I sent him a text. I told him I was sorry and that I missed him already. So just seven months after moving to Plano from Connecticut to be with me, he was gone. But was he really?

Chapter Eleven

A few days after Gabe left, I called him at work to ask him what he wanted me to do with his mail. I was surprised when he took my call. We talked for a few minutes and he said he would call me back after work, and he did. He said he still wanted to be with me, but he needed time to be on his own for a while. So we were on a break. I had no idea what that meant but I was happy we were still together(ish).

For the next month or so Gabe would come to the house on Tuesday, his day off, and on Sunday for the day. Around five he would take off and go back to where he was living. He had rented a room from a guy he worked with. His place was close to the gym he worked for and a good 50 minutes away from me.

We spoke, sent emails and saw each other when we could. I felt as if we were trying to work things out. When he told me he was going out I didn't question him in the way I used to. I didn't call him or text him as much. But it was on my mind all day, every day. I wondered what he was thinking. I thought about how I could prove to him

Kelly Smith

that I was not who I used to be.

Who was I? After he moved to Plano, I grew more and more needy. Codependent. At the time I had no idea this was what I was doing. I thought being jealous and wrapping my life up into his was what love looked like. I thought that knowing every step he took was my business; that I was entitled to know his every move. I was the same way with Derek and Derek didn't seem to mind. I figured this is what a relationship was. On the flip side, Gabe did the same things I was doing.

With both of us acting this way I never questioned freedom in a relationship. I always thought when you were in a relationship nothing and no one else mattered. You lived and breathed for each other. A strong sign of codependence, insecurity and neediness. The nights I sat home waiting for his call, waiting for him to choose me, I drove myself nuts. I figured if I courted him, he would see how much I loved him and he would come home. It was my mission to get him home.

You may be thinking, "wait, I thought he was awful." He was. We had an abusive relationship with each other. I reacted to the way he acted. I wrapped up my value in him. In him choosing me. If he chose me, I could be loved. If he didn't, then I couldn't. I was going to fight hard for him to choose me again.

One evening I was thinking about how much he missed his nephews. Family meant a lot to Gabe. I called an airline and booked flights for his two nephews to come to Plano and surprise him. Since they were both under thirteen, I had to get them on a direct flight from Connecticut. Only catch was I had to pick them up in Houston.

After booking the flights, I was happy. Excited. I had a great relationship with his nephews and I was going to surprise Gabe. I could see it now, Gabe rushing home to embrace me after he saw the email with the flight info, scooping me up and telling me he was ready to come home. Sound familiar?

The next morning after I sent the email, I eagerly waited by the phone for his call, for his pronouncement, but that never came. I received a text.

"I can't talk now, but thank you," the text read.

What? He can't talk? Why not? I was confused, but still excited. The kids would be here soon and we would have fun together. Or so I thought.

Something still seemed off. He never wanted to sleep over. We were having sex, but he never stayed over. I had been to his new place a few times.

The week after he moved out was Mother's Day. He called and asked me to come by to his new place and I did. Since Derek no longer acknowledged me on Mother's Day, Gabe always did. He gave me a card and a necklace of a crucifix. I loved both. We stayed there for a while and then we headed back to my house. I grew suspicious when we took separate cars. But I didn't question anything because things seemed to be going well. We went out to brunch that day with the kids and like clockwork, he left at 5 PM. This went on for about four weeks.

Around the four-week mark, I grew more and more suspicious of him and the way he was acting. He was no longer jealous or angry. It was hit or miss when he responded to my calls and suddenly he could no longer take my calls at work. On a Monday afternoon, I called a cookie delivery service and sent him his favorite cookies to the gym. He texted me to say thank you, but didn't call.

Sometimes he would invite me to the gym when

he worked nights and I would bring him dinner. He was looking to buy a new car, so he asked me to meet him at a nearby dealership so he could get my opinion and while there he introduced me as his girlfriend. At times like that I felt like things were going well and at other times I knew something was up, but I couldn't figure out what.

One afternoon, I had had enough. I got online and checked his phone bill. Two numbers stood out. I wrote them both down and I called them. One was his boss and the other did not have the voicemail set up. So I paid 99 cents to do a reverse lookup. Suddenly I had a name and an address. Tiffani Perkins.

"Tiffani Perkins?" I said the name out loud a few times. Who is she? Looking over the times they spoke and how often, it looked like a relationship. I looked back a month or so. They started talking before he moved out. I noticed a pattern. Her number for fifteen minutes, my number for four minutes and then hers again. He was talking to her and then hanging up to take my call and then calling her back.

I remembered a few months earlier when I called him while he was on his way home from work and he yelled at me. He said he didn't need to talk to me on his way home from work. He then hung up and we never chatted on his way home again.

I felt sick. Something told me to call the gym and ask for her. But I didn't. I called my friend from home and had her call the number. She did. Someone answered but said nothing.

So I called. She answered. I asked her if she was sleeping with Gabe Eriksson? She said no and I said "well, he's fucking both of us." She denied she was seeing him or talking to him and hung up.

I called Gabe. She must have gotten to him first because he put on this asshole act. When I got upset and asked him who she was, I insisted on knowing if she was sleeping at his place. When he said yes, I hung up. I was already on my way to his gym. I was sweating. Hurt. Angry. I had no idea what I was going to do when I got there, but I knew it was going to be big and I no longer cared. The entire car ride there my stomach was rotting. Butterflies now armed with grenades, guns, and bombs swarmed my stomach.

I pulled in and he was standing outside with a client.

He knew I was going to go there and he thought he was safe by surrounding himself with a few people. But like I said I no longer cared. I didn't give a fuck who he was with. I had questions.

He saw me and got into my car. I asked him about her and then everything was a blur. All I remember doing was hitting him, yelling at him and making him give me back the watch I had given him for our first Christmas. I snatched his phone and the watch and I made a run for it. I was running and he was chasing. We ran around the lot of the gym. When he got his phone back I smashed his watch on the ground. I cried and yelled at him. I announced he was a cheater and he could not do anything about it. I was sure he was pissed. Pissed at me for showing up. For figuring him out. For embarrassing him.

But in reality, he loved it. I looked like an idiot and he the victim of a crazy ex. No one knew the story yet, but they would. I got in my car and drove away. I cried all the way back home. I was so mad, so hurt. When I got home I decided I was done with him. Finally. I was walking away.

Then, my phone rang. It was Tiffani. She told me

they had been seeing each other for over a month. He told her he loved her, wanted a family with her, and was going to marry her. She told me he gave her a diamond necklace for her birthday and I asked her to send me a picture of it. When the photo came though, I was shocked to see he had given her my diamond necklace for her birthday, the day after he moved out. She told me that the day he left my house, they moved in together.

I was flabbergasted. I couldn't believe this was happening. I went from never suspecting him of cheating to finding out he was already living with someone. Everything started to make sense. Why I could only see him on his days off, and why I could only see him on Sundays. She had a kid she left with her mom during the week so on the weekend she would go see her kid. She returned on Sunday evening.

That night Gabe called me. He asked me if he could talk to me when he got out of work and stupidly, I said yes.

We talked about what was going on. He told me she was just a fling, she meant nothing. I told him about the conversation we had, the necklace, the things he said to her about being in love and wanting to have a family with her. He insisted he never said those things. He insisted he never cheated on me.

I asked about details, all of the details. I wanted to know everything about her. She was younger, about thirteen years younger. She had a daughter she didn't live with; her mother took care of her. I asked how long this was going on. His response didn't really matter, I had phone records so I already knew, but I wanted to know what he would say. He knew I had the proof with his phone records, but he told me they only talked as friends first. That he didn't feel anything for her but over time he grew feelings for her, but they were not serious feelings. We talked for awhile and I began to believe what he was saying. We talked about his nephews coming to visit, and he said he would stop seeing her.

But over the course of the next few days, I found her social media and things began to unfold. He forgot to mention she worked with him. That was not good. She was the front desk girl at the gym. They started talking at work when she was hired a few months before the phone conversations began. They flirted and met for drinks.

They talked and got to know each other until one day they took it further and began to talk and meet outside of work, alone.

The pieces started to fit. The late nights, the not coming home, his password changing and the fights he would pick for no reason, just so he could storm out. After putting the pieces together Gabe and I met and talked about all of it again. I was ready to forgive. I was ready to be with him again and forget all of it. Now I had competition and I had to win. I told him with the kids' trip coming up if he did not fully end it with her, I was walking away. He said he ended it and I was happy. I was worried because they worked together but from what he said she said she was going to quit her job. She didn't quit.

One evening when Gabe and I spoke he told me he was going out with his coworkers and invited me along. I jumped at the invitation. They were headed downtown and I was along for the ride. In the car were two of his coworkers—the one he lived with and the other I had just met—Gabe, and me.

As we drove we all talked. It was weird because everyone knew he had been with Tiffani and they knew he had cheated on me with her. I can't imagine how that looked to them. I can't imagine what they must have been thinking. I made a joke about it to break the ice and that seemed to help a little.

Gabe and I go way back, I told myself. We go back twenty-plus years. Back home, Gabe has a reputation for having a short fuse. Not many people in this new life of his knew about this reputation. But I knew how to calm him. Handle him. Since we had been in a relationship for a long time, I could tell when something would set him off. I was used to the eggshells I walked on and they were in a way comfortable to me.

As we parked and walked out of the garage, Gabe grabbed my hand. We went to a few bars, a few nightclubs, and we had a lot of drinks. I was still angry with Gabe and so unsure of where I stood. I had no idea how to act. I felt happy to be with him, but I also felt stupid. So I was on the fence. I knew not to talk to any guys, so I didn't. But I did talk to the guy he lived with, Pablo. Pablo and I chatted a bit about the Tiffani situation when Gabe went to get drinks, but as I would see him coming back, I stepped away from Pablo and he had no idea why. I could tell it bothered Gabe when Pablo and I were talking but the more I drank, the more I didn't give a fuck. The more I drank, the more pissed off I got. And by the end of the night, we were all drunk.

Walking back to Gabe's car in the garage, everything seemed normal. Gabe held my hand and kept me close. His coworkers walked and talked and laughed in front of us. His one co-worker, Scott, super quiet, hadn't had as much alcohol so he was going to drive us back to Pablo's house. Gabe unlocked the car, opened the back door for me to get in and closed it behind me. Pablo got in the passenger side and Scott, the driver's seat.

Gabe got in, shut the door behind him, and then his hand was grabbing my neck. His face was close to mine, the alcohol on his breath was entering my nostrils, and his grip was tightening. While squeezing my throat, he yelled at me through his teeth. He told me when I was with him, I was with him I was not to talk to any guys when he was around. I grabbed his hand and tried to loosen his grip, but couldn't. I kicked the seat in front of me instinctively and Pablo turned around and tried to get Gabe to let me go. Pablo pleaded with him, Scott said nothing, and Gabe told him to turn around and to mind his own business. When Pablo would not listen to him, Gabe warned him one more time. Pablo called his bluff and I prayed to God that Pablo would leave Gabe alone. I knew what was coming if he didn't.

Suddenly Gabe let me go and went for Pablo. Blood was all over the front seat and within seconds Gabe was out of the car and had Pablo on the garage floor, kicking the shit out of him. Pablo wasn't moving and Gabe got in the car, and I followed him. He tried to get me out of the car, but I was worried about him driving drunk so I stayed in the car as we left Scott and Pablo in the parking garage. He drove off and headed to Pablo's house.

On the way there I yelled and cried. He was pissed and he started to hit me. Punching me in the chest, stomach, and arms as he drove. I tried to block his hands and his punches the best I could. He became more and more angry. Blaming me for what he did. I stopped crying and yelling and got in defensive mode. At one point, he grabbed my hair and my head, and I thought to myself, "He is going to kill you, do not go down without a fight." I swung my leg around and I kicked him in the face. In the eye. He called me names and then didn't say a word until we got back to Pablo's house.

He got out of the car and called Tiffani right in front of me. He begged her to take him back. He told her I was crazy. He said he loved her.

I got in my car and left. The next day I was home in my bed. I could hardly move. I was bruised up and I was sore. My phone rang. It was Gabe. He wanted to come over. I let him. His eye was huge. Swollen. Bruised. My body was as well. He came into my room and got into my bed and he hugged me. I hugged him back. We never talked about it. We spent the day together.

With him being there with me, I thought the call he made the night before didn't mean anything to him, until we were at dinner and he told me he wanted to be with Tiffani. I was shocked. He gave me the break-up speech and I thought for a second he was kidding. My stomach sank. And I held back tears.

Looking back on it, this was my out. This was the point where I should have walked away. I should have scooped up my dignity, dragged it home, licked my wounds and started to get over him. But I didn't.

This is where the love triangle began.

The nephews came to town when they were supposed to. Gabe came to my house to pick me up and we headed to Houston to get them. They were not arriving until the next morning, but we spent the night because they had an early arrival. The ride to Houston was a good one, until we got lost. Then Gabe was back. Eggshells were back. Tight chest was back.

When we got to the hotel he was not speaking to me because we had gotten lost. I rubbed his back until he fell asleep, and then I fell asleep. He was not ready to tell the nephews or much of his family about Tiffani. I am not sure if he knew what he wanted, but he didn't mention her too much to them at first.

The kids stayed with me the weekend they were in town and so did Gabe. I used the time to show him I loved him and the kids loved me and that I was a better fit for him. We fought on and off.

I could not control or hide my anger from him. He would text her and call her. They fought about him being there with me. He had planned on leaving to see her after the kids went to bed. And he did. He spent a few nights with me but then he left to see her. One of those nights with me we fell asleep and he woke up at 3 AM to his phone blown up and mine as well. She was looking for him.

That weekend we had fun with his nephews. When they left, I cried. I cried because I knew deep down I would not be able to be in their lives the way I had been. When I used to go home to see Gabe I saw them too. We went out to dinner, movies, and we ate whole cakes with just three forks. I grew to love them.

I cried for my loss. I knew they would always be in my life, but not in the same way, and that broke my heart. The drive back from the airport was awful. I got upset and yelled at Gabe. I am sure at the time it made his decision to be with Tiffani easier.

Up until she found out about me she never got upset with him. She had no reason to. And for him it was perfect. He could keep an eye on her at work, she left each Friday to see her kid, and she was back on Sunday evening. He had freedom.

With me, he had accountability. I had opinions. I questioned him. She didn't. She saw a handsome, smart, funny, charming man who said all of the right things at the right time, and he was interested in her. How could she not fall for him?

But how could I not fight for him? He told her that after his nephews left, he would not talk to me again, and she trusted him. I am sure he convinced her that I was a mistake and he screwed up and if she gave him another chance she would see who he really was: a great guy. I question why she stayed with him after finding out about me the same way I questioned myself. At the time I thought she was desperate. But Gabe is good at what he does. So the love triangle continued, for the next two years.

A few weeks after the kids left I leased a new house on the water. I had taken Gabe and the kids by the house to show it to them while we were on our way to ride ATVs. Gabe fell in love with it. He told me if I moved in he would move in with me. That made me happy, and it gave me hope.

But when the kids left I knew I needed to stop talking to Gabe. I tried to be strong. I withheld every urge to call him and I was doing well.

One afternoon while my son and I were driving

our U-Haul full of furniture, my phone rang. I knew the number. Gabe's gym. I thought twice about answering the call because he and I had not been talking for a few weeks and I was starting to feel okay about it, but I answered. It was a Saturday so I knew Tiffani was not there. He asked me how the move was going and I told him. After small talk he said he saw one of my friends in the gym and she was going to be there for a while. He knew I had not seen her in almost a year, so he wanted me to stop by. I did.

After I said goodbye to my friend, Gabe walked me to my car. As I got in it to go home, he kissed me on the lips and said he would call me later. My heart raced. I agreed he could call, and he did. He said things with Tiffani were not great and he missed me. We talked for a while and we agreed to meet so he could see my new house.

From there we met on his days off. He called me on his way into work and on his way home. On his late-start days we met, went shopping and managed dinners together. We didn't talk much about Tiffani, and when we did all we did was fight about her. He got mad when I questioned him about her and went days without talking to me. Then somehow, a piece of mail or an unsigned document always came up.

One day in the car I asked if he was going to stay with her. He never had a straight answer. And why would he? He had the best of both worlds. He had two girlfriends. I helped him with his work decisions, rubbed his back, and had intelligent conversation with him. She cooked and cleaned. And he had sex with both of us. If anyone was winning, it was Gabe.

I asked him to tell me if he planned on living with her and he said he would. Weeks later he got an apartment near me. And she was moving in with him. I found out and I freaked out. He said he had to live with her because he felt bad for her. She had been kicked out of her apartment with her friends and she was homeless if she didn't live with him. Made no sense to me at the time because she was already pretty much living with him at his friend's house. The way he explained it made him seem like a hero, saving her from homelessness.

I remember giving myself limits. "If he lives with her, I am done" was one of them. I was not done.

One afternoon while he was at work he called to say no one would be able to sign for his new furniture. I volunteered. He left the door open and I went in. I looked through everything. I looked through his iPad. I deleted his pictures of them. I dipped their toothbrushes in the toilet after I peed in it. I dumped out his vodka and replaced it with water and I mixed toothpaste with shampoo and conditioner. When the furniture arrived I had the movers put it in all in the wrong rooms. I knew she would be home first and she would have to fix it before he got there.

I was angry, but I didn't love myself enough to walk away. I was now, in a sense, staying to get back at her and to see if I could win.

From there the relationship continued. Friday nights he stayed at my house and he went back to his apartment on Sunday evenings. At times I was at his place while she was gone.

I tried to move on with my life. I forced myself to date, but I still loved him and I still had hope. I felt he was still mine and Tiffani was just in the way. But she felt the same way about me.

One night she called me. She wanted to know if we were still seeing each other. She suspected we were. She admitted he was mean. Called her names. Put her down.

And he was controlling. She told me she had been sick from their relationship. She had to see a doctor because she was throwing up from stress. He was checking her bag after she visited her daughter and he got mad at her for white shorts he said were too short for her to wear. When he saw things he did not like, he got upset with her.

And then he was walking in the door and she had to go. That night they fought and she moved out. He called me and we met up the next day. But within days she moved back in and stopped seeing her daughter. She began staying with him all weekend.

Things went on like this for a while. Gabe and I would go weeks without speaking, but something always brought us back together.

I think Tiffani and I were no longer fighting over a guy; I think we were fighting each other. Fighting to see who would win the prize. But the prize was a verbally abusive man who was also a cheater.

Even so, the times in between us seeing each other was a different story. On the nights he could not call, I fell apart. I wondered where he was. He was on my mind the entire night. If I had plans, I canceled them in case he called. I waited by the phone in hopes I would hear from him. I was sure to not be anywhere where I could not take his call in the evenings. I made sure to be awake in the morning so as not to miss his morning call. Most of our conversations were just listening to one another breathe.

But as the months grew longer and turned into years, it became more difficult to be without him and to imagine him with her. I imagined them being happy in their apartment, laughing, cooking together, and watching shows. I imagined them out at night with long romantic dances close together, surrounded by people applauding their relationship. Sundays were the most difficult day of the week for me to get through. At first he would come by on Sundays. He would cause a fight or lie about where he was going. We'd watch a movie, have dinner and then he would leave. At one point that stopped. He stopped coming over on the weekends. She was catching on to him and he began spending the weekends with Tiffani and her daughter. I only saw him during the week or if they fought. I was always his back-up plan.

The weekends were hard for me, but over time and with encouragement from my therapist I grew strong enough to not cancel plans, and a few times I didn't take his call. That empowered me. But I was only strong enough to not take his calls because I was drunk. I would pop a few pills and wash them down with whiskey. I would go days not only not thinking about him but also not knowing anything else about the weekend. That became a problem, especially when it came to a good friends' engagement party.

Years ago, before my divorce, Derek was busy running and coaching the football program in Plano. He was well known for volunteering and I was as well. We had a good group of friends from all walks of life.

One evening after practice was over, Derek and I were at a store. We saw the dad of a kid Derek was coaching. He owned a few restaurants in the area that Derek and I had recently visited and we did not have a great experience. As he walked toward us, Derek warned me to not say anything. Ignoring my husband's request, I approached Myles. Myles, a tall, dark and handsome type, was such a sweet guy, I would later find out. That night, I let him have it. I told him the problems with his restaurant and how to fix them. After a few minutes of bashing him, I walked away feeling very satisfied and Derek slowly put a bag over his head because he was so embarrassed.

I am not sure how or why, but Myles became a very good friend of mine. Soon after my divorce, I talked to Myles about it, how it happened, my roles and responsibility and how I was dealing with it. I opened up to him about the things I did wrong and he shared his own divorce experience with me. He told me he would never get married again because the hurt was too much, although Lola, the woman he was seeing and currently living with, was amazing. She was a perfect fit for him. She was secure in who she was, she was independent, successful on her own and she loved him for him. He just didn't want to be hurt again.

After that conversation, with me exposing my true identity, Myles still accepted me. He was still my friend and since then there is not a human I admire more. His acceptance of me meant so much to me, probably because up until then, I never really felt that accepted by anyone.

After a few years of living with Lola he produced an engagement ring and when I found out, I was hopeful. I was so happy for him. I called him and we talked about it. I told him how proud of him I was. If Myles was able to trust in love again, so could I.

It was during the love triangle that Myles and Lola held an engagement party. It was also during the time I was popping bottles and pills. That evening as I was getting ready for the party I was missing Gabe. I wished he could go with me. But I was going to meet a friend before the party for dinner and then make my way there. I opened up my pill bottle, took one, and headed out.

While at the restaurant I had a drink and then another. By the time I got to the party, I had already blacked out. I can remember only bits and pieces of that night, mostly because of the pictures I saw. That was first of many nights with my friends I do not remember. For years after that I introduced myself to people I had met four times already. After the fog cleared and I realized I had essentially missed the entire engagement party of my very good friends, I felt awful. Sad. At the time I had no idea I was so lost and miserable.

Other nights when I could not handle Gabe being away I drank at home alone. I visited wineries with my friends and bought the reds I liked in bulk. I took them home and on hard nights I filled my bathtub with water and bubbles. I'd turn my phone to Do Not Disturb, turn on my sad song playlist and get drunk. I'd be drunk in the tub, belting out the lyrics to Taylor Swift's most recent album. I carried on like this for a while.

One evening as I prepped my bath, I noticed I didn't have any more wine glasses. Taking a look around my over-sized Jacuzzi, I noticed the dirty glasses and the number of empty wine bottles all around it. I shrugged it off and polished off two bottles without using a glass. That same night, after my bottles were emptied, I crawled out of the tub. I forgot a towel. As I inched my drunk, crying body toward my bed, I looked at the time. It was 5:30 PM. I realized I needed help. I was done canceling plans. I was done being drunk all the time. I was done lying to my friends.

Over the next few days I started to realize the things I had shown up to but missed. Myles and Lola were such good friends of mine and I missed the party that meant the most to them. I had been letting my friends, my family, and myself down. But I had no idea what to do. I still loved Gabe. I still wanted to be with him and I was not going to let anyone or anything stop me from having him again. I felt that if I had him, I would be okay. If I didn't have him, I would not be.

Although I was drinking to forget him on the weekends and I knew it was becoming a problem for me, I was still not ready to let him go. I continued to see him, take his calls, and help him when he needed help. Anything from finances to taking him to the doctor when he was sick. I would pick him up, sit with him, and take him to get his meds. I made sure he had everything he needed and I checked in on him. When I had surgery on my foot, he showed up to see me and in the following days when I couldn't drive, he picked me up to get me out of the house. Flowers on my birthday, shopping spree for him on his birthday. When his parents visited we spent time together while Tiffani worked. We acted as if we were still a couple. Valentine's Day it was sapphire and diamond earrings for me and emeralds for her. He was living a true double life. And it was confusing to me. He was doing all the stuff I wanted him to, so why was he still with her?

One morning after he drove her to work in order to ensure she could not come home for any reason, I asked him why. Why are you still with her? He said he was attached. He never said he loved her, but he said he was attached. I walked toward the door and I looked back at him sitting on his couch, and I told him I had to walk away from him. He agreed. I opened the door, got in my car and cried my eyes out. I had to walk away. I could not do this to myself. I was miserable.

Tiffani had her suspicions but didn't want answers. And although I am sure he was torn, Gabe was still getting all of his needs met with two different girls. I was losing the most.

I got home, walked through my front door and started cleaning the kitchen. My phone rang. It was him. He had a question about a doctor's appointment. I answered it and he acted as if our conversation never happened. I took the call as hope, and he called because he was selfish. He was not ready to let me go that night; he called me like everything was normal.

A few weeks later was Thanksgiving. He and I talked about going home together. We thought maybe it was not a good idea and we talked about maybe it was time to just end things. We got into an argument about it and then we hung up. Thirty minutes later he called, saying he was going to go back home. I said nothing. He got angry and hung up. A few days later he was back in Connecticut with her. Another reaching-my-limit moment.

"If he introduces her to his family, I am done." I wasn't.

When I found out, I blew up his phone. I was pissed. He had never said it was that serious with her. Now she was there with him and his family. All I could see was red. I was so mad at him. So hurt and so confused that he would take her home with him. I called him and called until he answered. He was angry that I was calling and told me he would call me the next day. I was so mad I blocked his number. I took a few sleeping pills and went to bed. The next day he did call me. He called me and told he got arrested for a DUI the night before and he didn't know what to do.

"What am I going to do?" he asked.

"I don't know, ask your twenty-five-year-old girlfriend," I said.

"I am serious. What am I going to do?" he pleaded.

I told him I would call my lawyer, again. And I did.

Since he was still on parole, he needed permission from his PO to leave the state. He hadn't gotten that. Drinking while on probation was illegal as well. Since he was arrested in Connecticut he needed a lawyer there.

When he got home we met up. He was scared. He was afraid he was going back to jail. This was not my first rodeo with him. I sold my engagement ring to pay for a lawyer and I went with him to meet with his parole officer. It was a process, getting him through this. We talked a lot during this time.

I supported him, encouraged him, held him while he cried and made a plan for if he did go back to prison. I would pay his bills to make sure they didn't go to collections, pack up his belongings and deal with his car and apartment. At this point I was not trying to win anything, I just didn't want him going back to jail. I could picture his mom's hurt face if that happened and I hated that idea. I hated the idea of him going back, of him being alone.

A few months later he had the first of two court dates in Connecticut. I went home with him for the first date. It was during this court appearance that the judge was going to decide whether Gabe had a case to have his DUI charges dropped. We met with his lawyer in the courthouse and found out some of the charges would be dropped, but he still had one more that was pending and had to wait a few more months to hear about the judge's final decision. He still needed to see what the State of Texas was going to do with him for violating his parole. It was now up to the State of Texas to either send him back to jail or to discipline him in another way.

One night I was taking out my aggression with a friend on the track and my phone rang. It was Gabe. He was on his way home but he wanted to know if he didn't go back to jail if he could come home. I said yes. And we would find out in about a week's time. During that week I prayed. I was sleepless. I was worried.

The morning came. D-day. We got in Gabe's car and headed to see his parole officer. We walked in, showed our IDs, emptied our pockets and walked through the metal detector. Minutes later we were in the elevator saying nothing. Within an hour Gabe was a free man. He had to attend anger classes, wear an ankle monitor and pay a fine. We pranced to the car and headed to grab some food. Sitting in the car I was so happy. He was okay and coming back home.

I wondered how he was going to tell her. I wondered if she was going to go crazy. They still worked together so that was an issue but time would tell how much longer that would last. I sat back and enjoyed the ride. Twenty-five minutes later we pulled into a place near my house. As we walked in, he said he had to tell me something. I asked what it was but he would not answer. I lost my appetite.

I kept questioning him but he said he would tell me in the car. I pushed my food around as I watched him eat his. As we finished, he picked up the trash and threw it away. I stood up and for a moment I didn't want to leave the restaurant. Whatever he had to tell me was nothing good and if we stayed in the restaurant, much like the one we were in during the weekend when we got engaged, I would never have to know his news. I would never be hurt. While I was lost in my desire to never leave that local barbecue restaurant, he walked up behind me and opened the door.

We walked out hand in hand. As I got in the car I asked him again what he needed to tell me. He grabbed my hand once he was inside the car and he held it tight. He looked at me with those familiar green eyes, the same ones I fell in love with years ago. The ones with perfectly manicured eyebrows. But his face stone cold. His dimples, normally out and on display, were nowhere in sight. I looked at him and I met his eyes. He pulled my hand closer to his chest, rubbed his thumb along my hand, and I felt his heart racing.

He said, "She's pregnant."

Chapter Twelve

As I walked through the door of my first Celebrate Recovery meeting I looked around to see if I could spot a familiar face in the small crowd. My friend Jessica was supposed to meet me, but she had a reputation for running late so it wasn't a surprise that I had not spotted her yet. I slowly walked toward the crowd in hopes she would pop out with excitement upon seeing my face and seeing that I showed up. And like clockwork, I saw her smile rushing toward me.

Jessica threw her arms around me and guided me into the group. She introduced me to Melody, the group leader. Melody took me under her wing that night. She showed me around and helped me settle in. She walked me over to get a nametag, which I stuck to my shirt as we walked toward a table full of snacks and water bottles. She told me to help myself and we made our way through the group of smiling faces. She stopped to introduce me to everyone and I was greeted with handshakes, hugs, and warm smiles. When she told the strangers that I was a friend of Jessica's, they smiled wider, harder. Hugs were a little tighter. The hugs were nice, even from strangers.

Melody walked me through double doors that led to a large room with a stage, musical instruments, and chairs all lined up. To the left was a table piled with books and pamphlets. I scanned as quickly as I could in order to keep up with the tour. She wasn't rushing me, but I was trying to take it all in. As we walked she explained the meeting set-up to me. The first hour is a group meeting and the second hour was what she referred to as small groups of around six people. Men in one room, women in the other. After hearing the speaker of the night, I would meet up with her for a few minutes so she could explain more of the process to me. She led me over to a seat. I looked around the room and took it all in and thought to myself, "How did I get here?"

A few minutes later Jessica sat near me, but only for a minute. With her was her husband Matthew.

I had met Jessica years before this night. I met her while the kids were still small and Derek and I were still married. Derek and I were at the gym dropping the kids off at the daycare and Jessica was on a machine close by. With her large blonde curly hair and Patriots shirt, she got our attention. She noticed we also were sporting our favorite team across our chests and we hit it off from there. She and Matthew are both from Connecticut. Complete with thick accents, it was a friendship made in heaven. Over the next few years we saw them out and chatted. It wasn't until I got serious about competing that we became great friends.

Over the years I slowly opened up to Jessica about my private life. She listened and had good advice, but after the divorce and while I was seeing Gabe she started to mention Celebrate Recovery. She eased it into conversations like a slick ninja. And when the day came that I knew I needed help, Celebrate Recovery was the place I wanted to go.

The day Gabe first moved out was the day I knew I needed help. I knew I had to face my roles and responsibilities in the breakup of both my marriage and now my engagement. I was not an innocent victim of either. Yes, I should not have stayed with Gabe for as long as I did, but not all of this failed relationship belonged to Gabe alone. I had control issues. I was needy and I was codependent. I wrapped up my identity in both Derek and Gabe. To be fair I think they did the same, to different extents, and that's why both relationships lasted as long as they did. But I knew I could either blame everyone for my breakup and play the victim in the same way my mother taught me to, or I could face my own demons and get help.

It was not just the failed relationships that made me realize I needed help. It was also the relationship I had with my kids. On days I came home and they were in the living room, they walked upstairs instead of spending time with me. It wasn't until after Gabe left that I began to notice this.

During my relationship with Gabe, I had burned bridges with my friends and family and didn't realize it until he was gone. I am sure I would have lost people while I was married to Derek, but they stayed because they liked him. Most people just put up with my name calling, shaming, and put-downs of him. When I noticed I was doing the same things with Gabe, I backed off, but not entirely. Derek had it worse, but Gabe had his fair share as well. I needed help.

It wasn't until after I discovered Tiffani existed that I attended my first meeting with Celebrate Recovery. I called

Jessica and without question, she sent me the address and the time to be there and I was. That first night was the first night of the rest of my life.

At first I was there just to impress Gabe. I felt that maybe if he saw I was getting help he would love me again. But then I stayed for me. I stayed because the program was working for me and I let it. I let myself see who I was and I knew in order to be happy I had to change. During my time in recovery I was faced with my demons; codependency, insecurities, anger, resentment, narcissism, and control issues. Why I was the way I was. I was torn down, ripped open and slowly put back together. Scrambling to figure out which pieces went back in and which ones to throw away.

During this time Jessica and I grew close. She became my sponsor and supported me through it all. Through the twelve steps. Held me when I cried and screamed, "Why doesn't my mom love me?" "Why did Gabe leave me for someone else?" "How could I have been so mean to Derek?" She helped me get through tough times in my past, face my abandonment issues and she helped me admit things I had no interest in admitting.

In a way it was a detox. A massive life detox, but instead of drying out in rehab, I did it while living life. I did it while I still saw and talked to Gabe. I did it while I took calls from my mom, still shaming me for wanting to live my own life. I made an effort to make recovery and getting better a way of life, not just a temporary pit stop.

This was a long and at times a painfully slow process. I went to the meetings on Monday nights. I saw both Jessica and Matthew there and they always eased my heart, and my fears, and made it easier to show up knowing I was never really on my own. Although they were my friends before, today they are more than friends. They are my rock and my soft place to fall as well. Seeing them there, knowing what I was going through while not many others did, helped me to be brave and strong.

It was in the small group meetings that I healed the most. A handful of women from all walks of life, in the same room, at the same time all being brave. All being strong enough to say they needed help. I was inspired by each of them and they were somehow inspired by me as well. It was during those meetings I was honest. When the other women heard my truths, I was not judged, but respected for my honesty. And I saw the other women in the same way. How brave we were, how bold. None of us meeting anywhere else, but coming together to help ourselves and we end up helping each other heal.

Not every meeting was easy. Actually, hardly any of them were easy. They were me pouring out my darkness, faults, hurt, insecurities and everything in between and hoping to leave them behind, and I did. With each meeting I grew stronger.

As of today I have been in active recovery for three years and I see my therapist on a monthly basis. I have successfully restored each relationship I damaged while I was with Gabe. I have forgiven him for things that happened between us and I am still working on forgiving myself for the mistakes I made. I am living a full, happy life. I have figured out how to surround myself with only good people. I have figured out how to walk away from any relationship that doesn't make me feel good. I can pick up on red flags from miles away, and I have learned that just because a relationship does not work that does not make me less of a person. I have learned to lean on my friends when I need them, but that I can also take care of myself.

My anger and codependency will always be a work in progress, but I can honestly say today I am a strong, secure, capable, independent woman who has learned a lot in this short life but will never forget the struggles it took to get to where I am today. My recovery program has saved my life, but only because I wanted it to. Only because I was brave enough to acknowledge I played a role in choosing to stay in unhealthy toxic relationships. Only I could make the changes I needed to make and I did. I had help along the way, but for the most part it was a long walk I needed to take alone and it was worth every step.

As of today all of my mistakes, bad experiences, and the good and the bad memories are in my rearview mirror. Now it's up to me to live any life I choose.

After discovering Tiffani was pregnant, it really didn't matter what Gabe wanted anymore. He was going to be a father to their child and no matter what, that was not going to change. At first he went back and forth about what he wanted. He talked about us being together and raising the baby, he talked about running away and leaving it all behind. He was not sure he loved her for her or if he was just attached. He often said if she didn't get pregnant, he would not stay with her.

But in the end, he chose to be with her, whether his feelings for her were love or because she was pregnant. The only thing he knew was that he wanted to be in his child's life. In order for him to do that, he felt like he had to be with her.

It took me a few months to wrap my mind around the entire situation. To say I was upset is an understatement. I was destroyed. During those few months Gabe and I still talked and saw each other, but not as often. We both had a lot going on in our minds and at times it was just easier to not talk. I knew what her being pregnant meant and that it was only a matter of time before he was completely out of my life.

Months later I came to terms with all of it. I was sick of crying. Sick of fighting. Sick of all of it. He called me one night, intoxicated. He and Tiffani had gotten into a fight and she moved out, again. As soon as she was gone, he called me and we talked about getting back together even though she was pregnant. Looking back on it today it sounds insane to even consider. It would have been inviting permanent drama into my life. Being with him while she was pregnant would have been the final straw that pushed everyone in my life away from me. My judgement was so clouded that I could not see the amount of damage being with him would have caused me. I took his call that night and he asked me to go to his house, so I did.

On my way over through the dark, rainy night, I knew this would be the last time I saw him in this way. In a way where we had "potential" of being together. I told myself I had to end this once and for all. I could not continue being the go-between for him when they broke up or got into a fight. I pulled into his driveway, parked my car and walked into his house. Since I had been there before I knew my way around even in the dark. I found the stairs on the right and took them up to his bedroom. I opened the door to his bedroom and saw him lying in bed.

As I walked over I took off my shoes and he lifted the blankets for me to get in next to him, and I did. We lay in his bed in the house he shared with Tiffani and I told him I could not do this anymore. He agreed. We talked about our relationship before Tiffani was in the picture. The things we did wrong and the things we did right. In that moment I was still wrapped up in the idea of loving him. I still could not see how destructive we were together. It was difficult to know I would not see him again. Parts of me never wanted to let go and the other parts rushed me out of his house and on with my life.

When I felt I was ready and all the words I needed to say to him were successfully out of my mouth, I got up and looked down at him. His green eyes looked sad and he didn't say much. I don't know if he didn't say anything because it was hard for him or if it was because he just didn't care anymore, but I looked down at him, ran my fingers through his soft blonde hair, kissed him one last time and let myself out. With a heavy heart and a happy mind, I got back in my car and made my way home again.

I was sad. I knew it was over and I had no idea what to do with myself. I had no idea if I could let him go. But I did. I made an effort every day to not call, email, or text. I began to live again, one day at a time. I met with my therapist, my sponsor, and attended recovery meetings as much as I could. I cried. I missed him and I let myself.

Then after the fog cleared I could see the abuse I endured clearly. I could see it before, but now with no contact, I was healing and putting the pieces of my life back together.

Today, living life without Gabe, I am free. I had no idea how much abuse was going on in my life. I had no idea how far out of my life I had pushed my family and friends. I didn't realize it, but one by one, people were dropping me from their lives. My sister, my brother, my friends all grew tired of seeing me struggle through a bad situation I put myself in, over and over again.

Once things with Gabe ended, I began to repair relationships in my life. I was lucky because everyone welcomed me back into their lives. I missed holidays and birthdays. I missed weddings and baby showers. I gained weight and my life was a mess. The hardest thing for me to do was make a call to my sister. My sister could not handle seeing me upset over a man who was so abusive. She was done with me not seeing my niece and nephew and she had to, in a way, cut me off. After talking to her she agreed to let me back in, but slowly. I worked hard on that relationship and I will never take any of my friends or family for granted again.

After I left Gabe's house that night we didn't speak again for eight months, until Christmas Eve.

Every Christmas Eve my friends and I had a tradition. Each year we draped ourselves in the latest pajama fashion and gathered for a fun night of food, drinks, and games. I hopped into the shower, and as my music blasted in the bathroom of my home, I got ready to see my friends and make some more Christmas Eve memories.

Downstairs after I was dressed and gathering my bag to leave my house, I noticed headlights bouncing off the windows in my living room. When I didn't hear a car door or anything, I continued to get ready. But just as I was about to leave through my garage, I heard a knock on the door.

Weird, I thought. The kids were with Derek tonight, and all of my friends were meeting me somewhere else. I hesitantly walked to the front door. Through the frosted glass, I saw a face. I assumed it was Derek. But as I opened the door, my heart, my jaw, and my stomach hit the floor. My mouth dried up, chest grew tight, and I looked for eggshells on the floor. Gabe pushed the door open and walked in.

Up until this night I had not seen Gabe in almost a year. He had moved about an hour away from me and we were now living separate lives. He showed up on that Christmas Eve because he missed me. Or so he said. He was driving alone on a long stretch of road when he took a call from his family back in Connecticut. With tears in his eyes as he stood in my living room, he said he was sorry for everything that had happened to us. That I was the reason he was still in Texas and he wished things had worked out between us and that he loved me. I wiped away the tears that gently fell from those green eyes and I hugged him. We talked for a few minutes and then he left.

As I watched Gabe's silhouette disappear down my front walkway, get into his car and head off into the dark, cold Christmas Eve night, I gently closed my door. The same door he so easily walked in and out of for the past few years. The door that is attached to the house we had planned to live in together until he derailed his own plans. The same door he had not walked through in almost a year. For what seemed like hours after and with his cologne still heavy in the air and on my shirt, I pressed my forehead against the door, closed my eyes, and whispered, "Motherfucker."

Gabe and I are no longer in touch. Some days I still miss him. I miss the parts of him that were good. Other days I can't thank God enough for removing him from my life. Mostly I don't think of him at all. I don't hate Gabe. I don't love Gabe. I want the best for him but I no longer want him in my life.

A few months back, Derek called me. He invited me to have lunch with him. I agreed and a few days later we met up at a restaurant. I knew what he wanted to tell me, and I was not 100 percent ready for it, but there is no stopping a train. We sat in a booth and ordered drinks. I looked across the table at him and asked him what was going on. He told me he was going to propose to his girlfriend Maude. He and Maude had been seeing each other for a year now and they were ready to make the big move. He was buying a house big enough for our kids, her two kids and them.

Although it wasn't a shock to hear him say this, it still stung. Parts of me always thought we would get back together. I am not sure if it's what I wanted or if it was just a fairy tale, but here he was, the father of my three boys, my partner in crime, my ex-husband and ex-best friend, telling me he was ready to move on with his life with someone else.

I knew I had put him through some pretty awful times while we were together, and since I had been in recovery, I was taught how to make positive changes in my life and that changed behavior is the best apology. I spoke of my fears; I told him I thought it was too soon. He explained how happy he was and that he felt that he was making the right decision. I could see a sparkle in his brown eyes I had not seen in a long time. I looked at him and told him I would support him no matter what he did. I would wish him luck and success in his marriage, and I would always be there for him.

We sat together for a few hours. We ate. Talked. Laughed. As we got up to leave I smiled a big smile at him. I had worked so hard in my recovery program so I could smile at him in the best moments of his life. We walked out of the restaurant and toward the cars. I forced a hug on him and told him I was happy for him, and I was. I was actually, truly happy for him. Since that day, he and Maude have married. They are working on blending the families and I am still supporting him and my kids as much as I can. Derek and I don't talk as much as we used to and at times I miss him too. But seeing him happy makes me happy and I can't ask for much more than that. We are successfully co-parenting our kids and I could not be happier with how both of our lives have turned out.

The relationship with my mother is, in a word, over. We no longer speak. Over the years she pushed me away to the point where I can no longer have her in my life. It has been over three years since we have communicated. She never had a relationship with my kids and now she doesn't have one with me. The last time we spoke I called her because I had just found out I was published for the first time. After I ended the call with the publisher of my article I said out loud, "She's finally going to love me."

I grabbed my phone and called her. When she answered she wasn't thrilled it was me, but I told her my good news anyway. This was my moment. The moment I was going to be loved and I could not wait for it.

"I have been published," the third grader in me said cheerfully.

"Is it about me?" boomed the now-unhappy voice.

My heart sank. My throat dried. And I said, "No it's not about you."

"You know the last thing I need is for the world to read something about me."

"It's not about you," I said, holding back tears.

"Then what. What is it. A recipe?" She snapped.

"No," I said. "I have to go." I hung up the phone and in that moment the adult in me took the tiny hand of the third grader living inside me and said, "I am proud of you. I love you."

I have not heard from her since. I have worked through all of the damage I was born into and all the damage I added and I am OK with living without her. It's not easy living a life never feeling the love of a mother, but not everyone is lucky enough to have a loving mom.

If you are in a toxic relationship, whether you're a man or a woman, there are steps you can take to successfully get out. First you need to admit you are in a toxic relationship, and that may be the most difficult step. Once you admit that, take your time and make a plan to leave. Talk to someone you trust. Let them know you feel you are in a toxic relationship and you are ready to leave.

Find a safe place to go, and go.

Once you are out of that relationship you need to get help. You need to find out why you were in a toxic relationship in the first place. A healthy person does not stay in a relationship that is harmful in any way, shape, or form. Find a good therapist. See your therapist weekly and possibly join a recovery group. I discovered Celebrate Recovery at my local church. Celebrate Recovery saved my life, but only because I allowed it to.

Do not date while you're healing from a toxic relationship. If you date too soon you will just keep attracting the same sort of partner. You need to heal yourself fully before you bring anyone else into your life. Yes, being alone can be scary, but being in an unhealthy relationship is worse. It is not easy, but you're worth it.

If someone you know is in a toxic relationship and refuses to see it, it is okay for you to walk away from that person. It can be stressful, exhausting, and annoying to talk to someone you love who keeps making the same mistakes over and over again. You can only say so much before it leads to the end of a relationship with you and your friend/family member. You have to take care of yourself first and sometimes leaving your friend/family member's life is the wake-up call they need to see that something's not right. If you can stay and support them that is great too, but remember there is nothing you can say, shout, or scream that will convince them to see what they refuse to see. Do the very best you can and let go if you need to.

Everything I have gone though, I have gone through to get to this point in my life. I wrote this to help you realize you are not alone. I opened up the darkest most private moments of my life to expose what an abusive relationship looks like. I hope friends and family of someone who is in a toxic relationship can understand a little better how manipulation works and how difficult it is to just walk away. For those of you who are currently in a toxic relationship, know that you will never be alone. You can get out of any toxic relationship and be okay.

Toxic relationships are not just romantic relationships. You can find a toxic relationship with your parents, siblings, extended family, and even friends. It is okay to let go of anyone causing you harm. Not all abuse is covered in blood, broken bones, or bruises. Be aware:

your kids know what is going on. Even the smallest child is aware. If you can't leave for you, leave for them. There is always hope, but you have to be the one who decides you deserve to be happy.

Gabe taught me lessons I would not have learned if it was not for him. Derek is now happily married. My sons are so much older and happy to have their mom healthy. I have healed so much and I am living a life my kids are proud of.

Take a chance on you. Be brave.

Acknowledgements

Edgar: Thank you for being 100% of who you are, every minute of every day. From when we met, through our marriage, divorce, and right to this very minute, you have been supportive, understanding even when I did not deserve it, and you never left. If not for you, there would be no me and vice versa. We rose from the ashes and created an amazing life for not only ourselves, but for our kids as well. I appreciate you and everything you do for me and our six brown eyes. Treelady xo

Jack, Harry, and Cain: My three sons, I know it hurts your hearts to read my story, but one day when you're ready, it will be here waiting for you. I hope when you finally do read my words, you find understanding, hope, strength, healing, and happiness within them. These words have been written for you. Long after I am gone, my words will remain to guide you in the right direction and I will never leave you alone. I love you guys. Always and Forever.

Kery: Seconds turned into minutes. Minutes turned into hours and those hours turned into almost four years of breaking down, discovering, facing, healing, and, eventually, living. I am living a healthy, happy, independent, successful, amazing life and none of this would have been possible if not for you. You believed in me enough to walk this journey by my side. You believed in me enough to sit next to me as I cried, screamed, and poured the toxins out. It is not easy to watch someone you love detox people out of their lives, but you did it. I can't thank you enough. I love you!

Stacie/Ruth/Pam at Sunny Day: For believing in me when I did not have the guts to believe in myself, thank you. Thank you for taking a risk on me and giving me a chance. I appreciate the positive support, hand-holding, and listening to me every time I called crying, and I cried a lot!! This book is something I never imagined possible. You have made my dream a reality and I will be forever grateful to you all!

Lorna, Steven, Hayden, Michelle: I know none of you would ever think about taking credit for anything I have accomplished, but if not for each one of you, your guidance and direction, ideas and honesty, I would not be where I am today. You each brought your own creativity to the table and each one of you impacted this project-turned-book in a positive way. It started with an idea and took off because each of you believed in me. Thank you for every second, minute, and hour that turned Signs in The Rearview Mirror into what it is today.

Mike: If it were not for your unconditional love, support, and encouragement, I not only would not have been able to write this book, but I would still have no idea who I was. You have shown me strength when I was weak, laughter when I was sad, and encouragement when I was down, but more importantly you have shown me what unconditional friendship looks like. Thank you for accepting me when you should have written me off. I could not have picked a better human to call friend. Thank you.

Sheri: From day one until now you have not only been by my side and my rock, but you lived it all with me. There is no one else I wanted by my side through this journey. For supporting me and encouraging me when I didn't deserve it, thank you and I love you.

Amy, Aaron: Times were tough. Hard. Painful. I know how difficult it was to see me go through all of this. I know at times it was easier to close your eyes than to see me suffer. If you didn't close your eyes at times, I may still be where I was. Thank you for letting go when you needed to but more importantly, thank you for letting me come back and fix what I broke. I love you more than you know and I would not want to be on this journey with any other siblings. I will never leave you guys again.

Miles: You inspire me to be a better version of me. I work hard to make you proud. For each time you hugged me, cheered for me just for walking through the door, and called me Aunties, I thank you. I love you and I promise to prove it every day!

Jeff, Tina, Laura, Tarryn, Jen, Darcie, Scott, Eric, Stacie, Lori, Dr. K, UrsV, Michelle, Deidra, Giulio, Auntie Donna, Johnny, Michael, Zachary, Hunter, Erich, Jeananne, Kylie, Pam, Jamie, Jodie, Sarah, Cooper, Tony, Melissa, Rebecca, Kerri, Jenn, Lisa and Monica and so many more: Thank you for reading, listening, sharing, hand-holding, putting up with my crying (some more than others), late night/early morning texts of desperation and always offering a kind word of encouragement for me when I had difficulty writing, but mostly for your unconditional support and love. Without friends/family like you, I honestly have no idea where I would be. Thank you!!

16468266R00118

Made in the USA
Lexington, KY
16 November 2018